The
ESSENTIAL
GUIDE
to
HEALING
WORKBOOK

Other Books by Bill Johnson

The Center of the Universe

Defining Moments

Dreaming with God

The Essential Guide to Healing (with Randy Clark)

Face to Face with God

Healing Unplugged (with Randy Clark)

The Power That Changes the World

Release the Power of Jesus

Strengthen Yourself in the Lord

The Supernatural Power of a Transformed Mind

When Heaven Invades Earth

Other Books by Randy Clark

The Biblical Guidebook to Deliverance

Changed in a Moment

Entertaining Angels

The Essential Guide to Healing (with Bill Johnson)

The Essential Guide to the Power of the Holy Spirit

Finding Victory When Healing Doesn't Happen (with Craig Miller)

Healing Energy: Whose Is It? (with Susan Thompson)

Healing Is in the Atonement: The Power of the Lord's Supper

The Healing River and Its Contributing Streams

Healing Unplugged (with Bill Johnson)

Lighting Fires

Power, Holiness and Evangelism

Supernatural Missions

There Is More!

Biblical Basis for Healing

Christ in You, the Hope of Glory

Evangelism Unleashed

Falling Under the Power of the Holy Spirit

Healing Out of Intimacy/Acts of Obedience

Learning to Minister under the Anointing/Healing Ministry in Your Church

Open Heaven/Are You Thirsty?

Pressing In/Spend and Be Spent

The Thrill of Victory/The Agony of Defeat

Words of Knowledge

MINISTRY MATERIALS

Ministry Team Training Manual

School of Healing and Impartation (SHI) Workbooks:

SHI Kingdom Foundations (Revival Phenomena and Healing)

SHI Healing: Spiritual and Medical Perspectives

SHI Empowered (Deliverance, Disbelief, and Deception)

BOOKLETS

Awed by His Grace/Out of the Bunkhouse

Baptism in the Holy Spirit

The ESSENTIAL GUIDE *to* HEALING

EQUIPPING ALL CHRISTIANS *to* PRAY *for the* SICK

BILL JOHNSON *and* RANDY CLARK

Chosen

a division of Baker Publishing Group
Minneapolis, Minnesota

Published by Chosen Books
11400 Hampshire Avenue South
Bloomington, MN 55438
www.chosenbooks.com

Chosen Books is a division of
Baker Publishing Group, Grand Rapids, Michigan.

Printed in the United States of America

ISBN 978-0-8007-9795-9

Cover design by Kirk DouPonce, DogEared Design

16 17 18 19 20 21 22   7 6 5 4 3 2 1

CONTENTS

ALL CHRISTIANS ARE CONDUITS

We can sum up our reason for teaming up to write *The Essential Guide to Healing* and this workbook to go along with it in one line: *More people get healed when more people pray for healing.*

Every Christian is a conduit through whom the Good News of the Gospel and the power of the Holy Spirit can flow to the world. That means God can use you to pray for the sick, and it is our hope that you will do exactly that after going through this study.

You can become a conduit for the healing power of God to flow to those in need. As you read *The Essential Guide to Healing* and work through the sessions ahead, you will gain both the scriptural foundation for that statement and the experience to back it up. That is our purpose and prayer.

We believe that all Christians should be equipped to pray for the sick. While it is true that some have a gift of healing, we all can be educated about how to pray for healing. We all can be ready to put that knowledge into practice when God gives us opportunity—and He will, if we are ready and willing!

The ministry of healing is not reserved for a select few. It is for *you*.

READY AND WILLING

How to Use This Workbook

Note: The recommendations in this section come from the editors of Chosen Books.

The Bereans, because they received the message of the Gospel with great eagerness and examined the Scriptures daily to see if what they were hearing was true, were called noble in the book of Acts (see Acts 17:10–12). The King James Version says they received the word "with all readiness of mind" (verse 11). Are you ready and willing, as the Bereans were, to learn all you can about important spiritual things? Are you eager to examine important truths about the healing ministry and experience those truths in action for yourself?

This workbook, which we have divided into different sessions that follow along with the chapters in *The Essential Guide to Healing*, is designed to take you through that process. As you work through these sessions, you will gain a solid scriptural and theological basis for seeing the gifts of the Holy Spirit in operation today, particularly the gifts of healing. You will understand your authority when it comes to the ministry of healing, and you will learn how to receive and relay words of knowledge related to healing. You will also be able to walk out healing ministry with greater boldness and effectiveness by implementing what we call the Five-Step Prayer Model.

Each session in this workbook is divided into four lessons. If you take a day or two to cover each lesson, you can get through each session in a week, a pace that lends itself well to either individual or small group study. To get the most out of the pages ahead, we suggest that you move through each lesson thoughtfully, taking your time with the readings from *The Essential Guide to Healing* and any accompanying Scripture readings. After you have read through the lesson and assigned readings, answer the questions that follow in "The Berean Approach" section. Pray that the Holy Spirit will give you insight and "guide you into all truth" (John 16:13) as you move through the readings and answer each question. He is in every way our "essential guide," ready to teach us everything we need to know and fully equip us to carry out His purposes and plans for us. Keep a ready mind and an open heart, as the Bereans did, and expect that God will use this study to make you more effective in delivering His healing power to those in need.

At the end of each session, you will also find a video guide with fill-in-the-blank questions you can answer while watching the video segments we have filmed to go with each session. While you can use *The Essential Guide to Healing* book and workbook to study this topic on your own, it would add greatly to your experience to purchase and view the videos as well. In each video we add more insight and clarification about each session's focus, and the videos are designed to enhance and complement the book and workbook.

The ideal would be to join—or even host—a small group study so that you and other believers can work through these materials together. In a small group setting, you can foster in-depth discussion about the readings, questions and videos, and you can encourage each other as you all grow your ability to minister healing. Within your group, there is even opportunity to practice the Five-Step Prayer Model and gain practical experience along with knowledge. If an *Essential Guide to Healing* study group is forming at your church or somewhere nearby, we urge you to join in. If no study group is available, consider putting one together. To help you do that, we have made available an *Essential Guide Curriculum Kit* for group leaders. It contains not only the book and workbook, but also the video segments and a special leader's guide that walks you through the steps to follow in organizing a study group and hosting the individual meetings.

RANDY'S JOURNEY

. . . I was in my office praying, "God, thank You that I'm not a liberal. I believe Jesus did what the Bible says He did. And thank You that I'm not a cessationist. I believe He still does what He did then."

I was expecting a "Well done, thou good and faithful servant with whom I am well pleased." But instead I heard from the Lord, "So what?"

"What do you mean, so what?" I quickly asked Him.

I heard, "You might as well be a liberal or a cessationist. It isn't enough to say you believe I still do what I did—if you don't know how to move in My gifts, you won't be able to do any more than a liberal or cessationist does."

This communication from the Spirit shook me. I determined right then that I would learn how to move in the gifts of the Holy Spirit.

Essential Guide, page 23

Day **1**

HOW I CAME TO BELIEVE IN HEALING

Randy

Now to Him who is able to do exceedingly abundantly above all that we ask or think, according to the power that works in us, to Him be glory.

Ephesians 3:20

God had spared me for a purpose. That was the only explanation that made sense about how I survived the major auto accident I tell you about in today's reading from *The Essential Guide to Healing*. Judging by the pictures of the car afterward (or what was left of it), clearly I should not have survived. Yet not only did I live, but God also healed me of numerous life-threatening injuries.

During my hospital stay, people prayed for me repeatedly and God would heal one thing or another (there were plenty of injuries to choose from). By the end of my ordeal, there was no denying that God had healed me in stages, miraculously and completely. I was able to leave the hospital several weeks before the doctors thought I would.

That experience, combined with a few other amazing miracles people close to me experienced, increased my faith and raised my interest in healing. That is how I came to believe in healing, and to this day, my faith and interest in it continue.

- Today's Scripture reading: Jeremiah 29:11–13
- Today's reading from *Essential Guide*: pages 9–20

The Berean Approach

1. I state in the book's introduction that to properly understand the subject of healing, one has to experience it. Think of a healing that you or someone close to you experienced. In what ways did that increase your faith and raise your interest in our topic?

   _____

   _____

   _____

2. By telling you the story of getting up out of bed after the doctors told me that movement could paralyze me, I was not suggesting that you defy sound medical advice on a whim when you need a healing. On what did I base my decision to get up? Why was that important? (See *Essential Guide* pages 16–17.)

   _____

   _____

   _____

3. Although the amazing experiences of some people close to me built my faith in healing, the death of my grandfather from cancer also introduced doubt. Have you had a similar experience that set back your faith in healing? What Scriptures or biblical principles helped you work through that?

   _____

   _____

   _____

Day 2

THE ISSUE OF MY LIFETIME

Randy

> Now about the gifts of the Spirit, brothers and sisters, I
> do not want you to be uninformed.
>
> 1 Corinthians 12:1

We cannot afford to be uninformed about the gifts of the Holy Spirit. We cannot afford to try to walk out God's plans and purposes without the Holy Spirit. Jesus made it clear to His disciples that they needed to wait until they received "power from on high" before moving out in ministry (see Luke 24:45–49). Moving in the power and giftings of the Holy Spirit is indispensable to effective ministry.

It is also highly controversial. I talk about that in today's reading from *Essential Guide*. I have seen enough controversy over the Holy Spirit to last a lifetime. In fact, the day I entered school on my way to becoming a preacher, the Lord told me, "The issue of your lifetime will be the Holy Spirit."

Why all the controversy? Because Christians believe *in* the Holy Spirit and know *about* the Holy Spirit, but knowing how to move in His gifts is a whole different thing! Once I saw firsthand how the operation of the Spirit affects people, the issue for me became the thought of living without that power in my life. Early on in my ministry, I reached a point where I determined that I had to learn how to move in His gifts. That determination set the course for the rest of my life.

- Today's Scripture reading: 1 Corinthians 12:1–11
- Today's reading from *Essential Guide*: pages 21–26

The Berean Approach

1. At what point did you determine that you had to learn how to move in the gifts of the Holy Spirit? What did you see or experience that compelled you in that direction? (If you have not yet reached such a point, I trust that you will by the end of this study.)

   ----

2. In today's book reading, I related the time when the Lord told me, "If you don't know how to move in My gifts, you won't be able to do any more than a liberal or cessationist does." Why isn't it enough simply to believe Jesus still does what the Bible says He did?

   ----

3. In the book I also related the time when the Lord told me, "I want you to include more of My words in your sermon, and less of your own." What effect might it have on our witness and ministry to others if we all included more of Him and less of us?

Day 3

FIRST IMPRESSIONS

Randy

I long to see you so that I may impart to you some spiritual gift to make you strong.

Romans 1:11

In the introductory pages of *Essential Guide*, I state that you cannot understand the subject of healing from the detached, unbiased position of a reporter. You have to *experience* it to understand it properly. As I tell you in today's book reading, that was what the healing conference I brought into my Baptist church was all about. From that life-changing conference, we formed our first impressions of the Holy Spirit in operation, so to speak. We experienced healing and words of knowledge and so many other manifestations of the Holy Spirit in ways that we as a church had never seen before, and to a much greater extent.

That conference left a lasting impression on all of us. It left us with a burning desire to learn more about how to move in the gifts, and it also left something else with many of us—an impartation to move in the Holy Spirit in new and increased ways. My impartation increased the words of knowledge and healings I could minister to others, and I continue to grow in those areas to this day.

Those impartations activated the Spirit's gifts in us, which made for some memorable experiences that still amaze me when I think about them. I think they will amaze you, too, as you read about them in the book.

- Today's Scripture reading: John 16:5–15
- Today's reading from *Essential Guide*: pages 26–29

The Berean Approach

1. When my wife fell to the floor under the power of God during our first healing conference, it was definitely outside anything she had previously experienced—or ever wanted to experience—with the Holy Spirit. As I said in the book, she had a great aversion to it until she experienced it for herself. What have you experienced with the Holy Spirit that perhaps you formerly thought was not genuine when you saw it happen to others? How did your experience change your perception?

   _____

   _____

   _____

2. How is an open vision like the one my friend Tom had different from a mental picture? (See *Essential Guide* page 28.) Why do you think I related the vision to the church when Tom said he did not know how to interpret it?

   _____

   _____

   _____

3. After we started that first Vineyard in Illinois, my key leaders and I were so serious about learning how to move in the gifts of the Spirit and pray for the sick that we drove many hundreds of miles many times to see people like John Wimber or Blaine Cook minister. In what ways are you seriously pursuing the spiritual growth you desire? In what ways do you look to this study of *The Essential Guide to Healing* to help you?

   _____

   _____

   _____

Day 4

DONUTS IN THE DARK

Randy

Therefore, as we have opportunity, let us do good to all people.

Galatians 6:10

Frying donuts in the dark is the perfect occupation if you want a job that is a long way from any kind of glitz, glamour and glory. Yet it was also the perfect occupation for me in which I could try out what I call my grand experiment, which you will read about in today's book pages.

As you can imagine, getting up in the middle of the night to fry donuts in the dark and train bakery workers was not my favorite job of all time. Yet it was a stepping stone to ministry in the location God was calling me to, and it was also a stepping stone in learning how to hear from God, pray and see people healed—especially unbelievers.

Why would I teach people in my church to pray for their co-workers if it doesn't work? I asked myself back in those days. *Shouldn't I make sure it works before I expect them to do it?*

Those questions were the basis for my grand experiment, and the results of that experiment went beyond anything I had expected or imagined. Again, the Holy Spirit surprised me (which I ought to be used to by now). So did the receptivity of unbelievers to healing prayer.

- Today's Scripture reading: Matthew 5:13–16
- Today's reading from *Essential Guide*: pages 29–33

19

The Berean Approach

1. Sometimes people think following God's call will involve numerous "important," high-profile steps all along the way, and then they find out they will be frying donuts in the middle of the night somewhere. What kind of steps toward fulfilling God's call have you taken that surprised you? Were you able to make the most of each step by finding ministry opportunities, as I did?

   _____

   _____

   _____

2. Have you ever approached an unbeliever at work or in public and offered to pray for his or her healing? What response did you get?

   _____

   _____

   _____

3. Although we will answer this question in further detail in chapter 4, why do you think I found unbelievers even more receptive to healing prayer than believers were in my grand experiment?

   _____

   _____

   _____

Session 1 Video Guide

1. The Lord told Randy, "I want you to teach that I still _____ today. . . . I want you to preach differently: _____ of My Word, _____ of yours."

2. Learning to heal involves learning the _____ of God's Word, and learning to _____ God's Word, and to see what God is doing and to _____ with God.

3. Randy told the Lord, "You give me a word of _____; I'll _____ it. I don't care who it's for!"

4. When the _____ touches people, the autonomic _____ _____ will sometimes kick in.

5. Unbelievers naturally think that if there's a God, He is _____ and _____, and He can _____.

6. Randy said, "What I found out in my Grand _____: It _____!"

7. You carry the good news of the _____ of another _____.

8. In the name of that King Jesus, you have _____ and _____ to heal the sick.

BILL'S JOURNEY

Healing is often said to be mysterious. I agree. But Jesus is not complicated. He made His will quite simple, saying "on earth as it is in Heaven" (Matthew 6:10). When people come to me for healing and they leave the same way they came, I pray like this: *Father, they came to me expecting to encounter Jesus, and all they got was me. And neither of us is impressed. You've got to work deeper in me so that when the multitudes come to us, they get more than a Bill encounter.*

We started in all of this by crying out to God in private and taking risks in public. Those are essentials in healing, and they have never changed through the years. Taking personal responsibility to do the impossible is the only way I can honestly face my responsibility to represent Jesus. In Matthew 10:8, Jesus did not command us to *pray* for the sick. He commanded us to *heal* them.

Essential Guide, pages 50–51

Day **1**

INADEQUATE AND UNQUALIFIED?

Bill

Then Peter opened his mouth and said: "In truth I perceive that God shows no partiality. But in every nation whoever fears Him and works righteousness is accepted by Him."

Acts 10:34–35 NKJV

Do you ever feel inadequate and unqualified to accomplish great things for God? I once experienced that feeling regularly myself. Even though I grew up in a great Christian home with fantastic role models, I spent much of my early life feeling as if I could not quite measure up spiritually. As I tell you in today's reading from *The Essential Guide to Healing*, I spent a lot of time comparing my "normal" Christian self to the spiritually "special" people I heard about or saw firsthand who were doing great things for God.

For a long time, I felt as if there was nothing spectacular about my relationship with God, and nothing significant seemed to happen when I would try to operate in the gifts. Yet I knew that miracles were an integral part of the Gospel message, and even into my first pastorate, I wrestled with the thought that I was unqualified to take part in them. My cry of inadequacy warred against my cry to experience more of the power of God.

There was one thing, however, that flowed from me effortlessly— worship. My father was a pastor, and he taught us as a church to worship. I continued that focus after I became a pastor. It was worship that led me into a deeper understanding of the anointing and moving of the Holy Spirit. In the presence of God, our inadequacies fall away.

- Today's Scripture reading: Isaiah 55:8–11; John 14:12–17
- Today's reading from *Essential Guide*: pages 35–41

The Berean Approach

1. What is the difference between knowing in your head that God talks to people in His Word and learning it in your heart?

   _____

   _____

   _____

2. I mentioned in today's reading from *Essential Guide* that it was godly peer pressure that convinced me I could give my all to God and love Him with all my heart. What effect has godly peer pressure had on you?

   _____

   _____

   _____

3. I developed some misconceptions about the ministry of power that caused me to feel inadequate compared to the "special" people I saw operating in the gifts of the Spirit. In what ways have you struggled with this, as I did?

   _____

   _____

   _____

4. God can use our experience of lack to summon us into a deeper relationship with Him. What do you think it means to say that sometimes we need to fear lack more than we fear excess if we really want a breakthrough?

   _____

   _____

   _____

Day 2

THE RISK FACTOR

Bill

Heal the sick, raise the dead, cleanse the lepers, cast out demons. Freely you received, freely give.

Matthew 10:8

There is a time to learn and grow, and then there is a time to put a demand on what you know. After I attended two John Wimber conferences, I decided that while good theology is important and I had it, it was time to add some experience to what I believed. I came home and started taking risks.

I looked at it this way: Our church was already in a place where we weren't seeing much in the way of miracles, so what did I have to lose by adding the risk factor? You probably have heard the saying "You get what you pay for." As a pastor, you also get what you preach. That thought compelled me to teach a midweek class on healing in which we became copycats. We copied whatever we saw that worked on every healing video we watched.

I tell you more about that in today's book reading, and no one was more surprised than me when it worked and we started to see breakthrough. But it would not have happened without adding the risk factor. Had I come home and done nothing after those conferences, I would have seen nothing as a result. Suffering a holy dissatisfaction can be a good thing!

- Today's Scripture reading: Joshua 1:6–9
- Today's reading from *Essential Guide*: pages 41–45

The Berean Approach

1. When I realized that my risk factor had to line up with the boldness of my beliefs, an immediate change came in my ministry. Why do you think it worked that way?

2. How is it that copying others can be the way we find out how our gift works?

3. Instead of making what God is doing the main thing, a lot of times we add what God is doing to what we are doing. Have you seen that happen? How does it prevent increase? (See *Essential Guide* page 44.)

4. Has God ever shaped you through hunger? What was your response, and what was the result?

Day **3**

MARKED FOR LIFE

Bill

Therefore I urge you, brethren, by the mercies of God, to present your bodies a living and holy sacrifice, acceptable to God, which is your spiritual service of worship.

Romans 12:1

Sometimes the presence of God is so sweet and peaceful. That had always been my experience with Him—deep and meaningful, but subtle, almost to the point of seeming uneventful. As I told you in the previous lesson, however, I hungered for so much more, and God shaped me through that hunger. I cried out for more of Him day and night.

When the more from God came my way, it literally blew my fuses. I describe its intensity in more detail in today's book reading, but at the time, I was certain I would never recover from it physically. It happened in bed, and thankfully, when I got up the next morning I was refreshed, not incapacitated. That was quite a relief!

That experience marked me for life. And in it, I made the choice to have more of God at any cost. No matter what I had to do or yield in exchange, the trade would be worth it.

- Today's Scripture reading: Matthew 13:44–45; 2 Corinthians 4:7–10
- Today's reading from *Essential Guide*: pages 45–47

The Berean Approach

1. Has God ever answered your prayer in seed form? How did you recognize the answer when it came, and how did it grow and manifest itself in your life?

   _____

   _____

   _____

2. I state in today's reading that some of the most important things that happen to us are the most difficult to explain to others, even though they are undeniably from God. What has God brought into your life that has been difficult to explain? How did people react when you tried?

   _____

   _____

   _____

3. What does it mean to say that sometimes favor from heaven causes problems on earth? Can you think of other scriptural examples besides Jacob's limp and Mary's encounter? Can you think of an example from your own life?

   _____

   _____

   _____

Day **4**

RESPONSIBLE TO REPRESENT JESUS

Bill

And great multitudes followed Him, and He healed them all.

Matthew 12:15 NKJV

I say this in today's book reading, and it is worth saying twice: I am not looking to feel good about myself. I am looking to be like Jesus. I must accurately represent Him until I can ac-curately *re-present* Him.

Jesus set the standard for us when He came, not only in the area of healing all who came to Him, but in every area. If we do not yet meet that standard, the lack is not on His side of the equation. The more we look like Him and represent Him accurately, the closer we come to seeing Matthew 6:10: "Your Kingdom come. Your will be done, on earth as it is in heaven."

Because of my desire to see that become a reality, I take personal responsibility to represent Jesus as accurately as I know how and to do the impossible for Him. Daily I pray for Him to work more deeply in me so I can meet His standard rather than lowering it to meet my experience.

- Today's Scripture reading: Ephesians 3:14–21; 1 John 3:1–3
- Today's reading from *Essential Guide*: pages 47–51

The Berean Approach

1. What is the greatest thing we can do to see an increase in signs and wonders? (See *Essential Guide* page 49.)

   _____

   _____

   _____

2. In today's reading I told you about the exponential effect my co-author, Randy Clark, has had on my growth and that of Bethel Church. Who in your life has had that kind of effect on you? What is it about their representation of Jesus that draws you?

   _____

   _____

   _____

3. What are two essentials in healing that have never changed? (See *Essential Guide* page 51.) Why do you think those two things so powerfully affect the results we see in healing ministry?

   _____

   _____

   _____

Session 2 Video Guide

1. Any kind of ministry at all that's _____ happens because of the Spirit of God _____ upon, _____ through, a believer.

2. We were created as a people to _____ and to _____ and to _____ God.

3. We always become _____ the one that we _____.

4. It would be _____ for us to think that the miracle anointing and the miracle assignment were _____ for the twelve apostles.

5. Bill said of those he learned from, "These great men of God and women of God were _____ something that could be done by _____."

6. Regarding revival, Bill said, "God lights the _____ on the altar, but it's the priests who keep it _____. . . . God is the one who _____ the move of God, but it is up to the _____ of God to keep it going."

7. Anytime _____ enters into a move of God, that's when the move of God begins to _____ _____.

8. Bill prayed, "God, if You'll touch me again, I'll never _____ the subject. I'll never try to _____ what You're doing to what we're doing."

9. Bill said that healing "is becoming an _____ grace to _____ all over the world."

10. Bill has found that one of the keys to increasing in healing is this: In private, _____ _____ to God. In public, take _____.

11. Courage says, "I'm going to _____ for the breakthrough in private, and then I'm going to _____ the breakthrough in public."

12. Bill said, "My personal motto is that I fear _____ much more than _____."

THE GIFTS
OF THE SPIRIT TODAY

Randy

Our study of the Scriptures conclusively indicates that the function or purpose of healings and miracles was to be part of the expression of the Gospel. The sign gifts were to continue until Jesus' Second Coming because they were part of the Good News about the inbreak of the Kingdom. They are the energies of God that make the power of God, as well as the presence of God, tangible today. They are the means by which the strong man's house is plundered (see Matthew 12:29). They are part of the Gospel and should accompany it. They confirm the Gospel.

Essential Guide, page 82

Day **1**

THE INBREAK
OF THE KINGDOM

Randy

God anointed Jesus of Nazareth with the Holy Spirit and
with power, who went about doing good and healing all
who were oppressed by the devil, for God was with Him.

Acts 10:38 NKJV

Perhaps you come from a liberal or cessationist background,
or perhaps you are new to the idea of the Holy Spirit moving in power in ways you have only read about in Scripture.
Whatever you believe or have been taught, I ask you to bear with me
through this session as I talk about why I believe the sign gifts are
active and available to every Christian today. Consider with me the
scriptural and theological foundations on which my co-author and
I base our belief, and like the Bereans in Acts 17, whom I admire,
examine the Scriptures with me to see if these things could be true.

I see the gifts of the Holy Spirit as the blessing of God's power
to help us in life *today*. They push back the powers of darkness and
plunder the enemy. They are signs of what I call the "inbreak of
the Kingdom," as the Holy Spirit manifests in the earth *today*. The
Kingdom breaks in wherever the Holy Spirit breaks out.

Here are the questions we will ask in the days that make up this
important session: Do the Scriptures teach that the sign gifts are
perpetual and therefore active until Jesus returns, or did they end

with the death of the apostles? How important are the gifts to the preaching of the Gospel? Were the apostles the only ones who worked signs and miracles, or were the gifts for all? We will make these questions, debated among Christians for centuries, our focus, and the answers we find will lay the groundwork for every session that follows.

- Today's Scripture reading: Romans 1:16–17; Hebrews 13:7–9
- Today's reading from *Essential Guide*: pages 53–60

The Berean Approach

1. My wife, DeAnne, and I have found that the gifts of the Spirit go beyond their theological ramifications to have very practical applications. What practical applications have you discovered if you currently operate in the gifts? (If you do not, be prepared to begin realizing some practical applications as you make your way through this study.)

2. What does the phrase "inbreak of the Kingdom" bring to mind for you? (See *Essential Guide* page 57 for what it means to me.)

3. What does it mean to say that the gifts are given more as a benefit to us than as evidence of correct doctrine? (See *Essential Guide* pages 57–59.)

4. Were you surprised by Dr. Jon Ruthven's results when he studied how much of the New Testament was written by the apostles? What does the fact that so much of the New Testament was

written by non-apostles say about the purpose of the gifts? (See *Essential Guide* page 58.)

Day 2

GLORY, POWER AND FRUIT

Randy

Therefore you do not lack any spiritual gift as you eagerly
wait for our Lord Jesus Christ to be revealed.

1 Corinthians 1:7

When we read the words *glory*, *power* and *fruit* in Scripture, we usually have in mind just what we think they mean. Often, however, our understanding is limited. If we understood their meaning fully, there would be a lot less debate about whether or not the gifts of the Spirit are perpetual.

Today's book reading is longer than most because in it we take a close look at the meaning of these three words in some key Scriptures. I urge you to read today's pages in *Essential Guide* thoughtfully and prayerfully, especially if your prior understanding has been that the Holy Spirit's gifts are no longer operational. This lesson on glory, power and fruit is foundational to my teaching about the Holy Spirit and His gifts in operation today.

I think once you work through this lesson, the words *glory*, *power* and *fruit* will take on a whole new meaning for you, as they have for me as I have studied them in depth. But this lesson will do more than increase your knowledge of our topic. It will position you to experience the Holy Spirit's gifts for yourself in a whole new way as you move through this study. And although the saying "knowledge is power" may not originate in Scripture, in this case it certainly applies!

- Today's Scripture reading: John 15:1–17; James 5:13–18
- Today's reading from *Essential Guide*: pages 60–72

The Berean Approach

1. How is it that both cessationists and noncessationists can use the verse 1 Corinthians 13:10? (See *Essential Guide* page 61.) Which usage illustrated your understanding of the verse before going through this lesson?

   _____

   _____

   _____

2. What was the number one way God received glory in the Bible? (See *Essential Guide* page 62.) How does this help us see the necessity of all the gifts continuing until Jesus returns?

   _____

   _____

   _____

3. In today's reading I state that the "fruit of righteousness" does not refer to righteousness itself or to salvation. What two kinds of fruit does it refer to? (See *Essential Guide* pages 65–66.)

   _____

   _____

   _____

4. What does it mean to say that the gifts were part and parcel of the Kingdom and confirmed the message, not the messengers? (See *Essential Guide* page 70.) What bearing does that have on the necessity of their operation today?

   _____

   _____

   _____

5. In light of the fact that the various gifts reflect various forms of grace, why doesn't it make sense to say that some of the gifts have ended? (See *Essential Guide* page 71.)

_____

_____

_____

Day **3**

FULLY PROCLAIMING
THE GOSPEL

Randy

I have fully proclaimed the gospel of Christ.

Romans 15:19

By all means, proclaiming the Gospel of Christ means bringing the good news of salvation, the forgiveness of sin and redemption to its hearers. But *fully* proclaiming the Gospel goes beyond even that astoundingly good news. Salvation in its fullest sense also ushers in healing and deliverance from demonic strongholds. That takes the power of God at work alongside the message.

Romans 1:16 tells us that *the Gospel is the power of God*. If the only lens we have ever seen that through is the reformational lens of salvation from eternal damnation, it is time to get our prescription checked and get some new lenses. The preaching and the power go together; the message and the miracles team up to proclaim that the Kingdom has come and is present here and now.

Power goes with proclamation—which is the title of the book section that makes up today's reading.

- Today's Scripture reading: Luke 9:1–6; 10:1–9
- Today's reading from *Essential Guide*: pages 72–77

The Berean Approach

1. How do you think it is significant that although there are hundreds of promises in the Bible, there is only one "promise of the Father"? (See *Essential Guide* page 73.)

_____

_____

_____

2. When you look at "much grace" in the context of Acts 4:28–33, what meaning do you see? (See *Essential Guide* page 74.)

_____

_____

_____

3. What does it mean to say we must be careful that our preaching does not appear to indicate that we are serving the "I Was" or "I Will Be," but that we are serving the "I AM"?

_____

_____

_____

4. What is your answer to my question on page 76 of today's book reading, "Can we believe we have *fully* proclaimed the Gospel of Christ when signs and miracles are not accompanying the preaching?"

_____

_____

_____

Day **4**

POWERFUL "LITTLE OLE ME'S"

Randy

Then the disciples went out and preached everywhere, and the Lord worked with them and confirmed his word by the signs that accompanied it.

Mark 16:20

I believe Scripture clearly demonstrates that operating in the power of God was not exclusive to the apostles. I believe it included the rank and file of the Church, the "little ole me's" who were not listed among the apostles, but who were listed in Scripture as those who also went out to preach and to heal. We will look at several examples of that in today's reading from *Essential Guide*.

We will also look at why you and I can be counted among the "little ole me's" who will do the same miraculous works that Jesus did. But first we have to get past our theological education problem. When it comes to our discipleship, many of us have mistaken *studying the Master* for *becoming like Him*. Observing Him and actually doing what He did are two completely different things.

The more we actually become like Him and obey His commands, the more the power of the Holy Spirit will be at work in and through us to do what He did, including healing and deliverance. There is no doubt about it—becoming like Jesus and obeying what He commanded will turn you into a powerful "little ole me."

- Today's Scripture reading: Matthew 12:25–32; Hebrews 2:1–4
- Today's reading from *Essential Guide*: pages 77–85

The Berean Approach

1. Why does translating "to obey" as "to observe" in Matthew 28:20 miss the mark of Jesus' intent? (See *Essential Guide* pages 79–80.)

   _____

   _____

   _____

2. What is the result of replacing becoming like Jesus with simply studying Him?

   _____

   _____

   _____

3. How does Dr. Wayne Grudem answer the assertion that miracles were primarily done by the apostles? (See *Essential Guide* page 81.)

   _____

   _____

   _____

4. The gifts of the Spirit are not limited to evidential purposes. What is their primary purpose? (See *Essential Guide* page 83.)

   _____

   _____

   _____

5. At the end of today's reading I tell you about an experience I had that demonstrated the beneficial nature of the gifts in real life. Have you (or perhaps someone you know) had a similar experience? How did it demonstrate in a tangible way the beneficial nature of the gifts?

   _____

   _____

   _____

Session 3 Video Guide

Col 112
1 Thes 5
11-13 ...
2 Thes 3 gift of
faith
Heb. 2 3 B+ H
Luke 9 1-2
" 10:17
" 24:49
Acts 1:8
" 3:12
Col 1:29

1. The gifts are the _blessing_ of God's power to _✓_ _help_ us in life.

2. There is a big _difference_ between the Gospel and all of our systems of _doctrine_

3. Out of the twelve apostles, only three _wrote_ Scripture.

4. Randy said, "I have this understanding of the Kingdom—that it ends in _greatness_; it ends in _power_; it ends with great _victory_."

5. You cannot give it (Scripture) a _meaning_ that would have made no sense to its first _audience_ ~~believers~~

6. Oil was not meant to be seen as _medicinal_, as some commentators say. It was _symbol_ of the Holy Spirit for Protestants and _sacramental_ for Catholics.

7. In Matthew 22:29, Jesus talks about two ways of being in error. One is not knowing the _scripture_, and the other is not knowing the _power_ of God.

8. The Gospel is the power of _salvation_ which means not just going to heaven, not just being forgiven, but also having the ability to work in _signs_ and _wonders_

9. The signs and wonders are given to _accompany_ the Word, not just the _apostles_, but the Word itself.

10. Randy said, "Not only do I know it from Scripture; I know it from _experience_. God uses _everybody_. Let God use you!"

Math 28:18-20
healing + deliverance
Math 13: 31-32
13:33
Rom 11:29
I Cor 1:7
" 13:10
" 14-21
Gal 3:5
any to "
Ephes.
Ep. 4 11:13
" 4:30
" 5 13
" 6 10-18
Phil 1 9-11
James 5 elders
James anoint sick

not term insurance
whole life

UNBELIEVING BELIEVERS AND BELIEVING UNBELIEVERS

Randy

Theologically speaking, the American and European Protestant churches have been bastions of skeptical unbelief toward healing and miracles happening today. That skepticism was taught to their members. My own experiences in college and seminary have caused me to see such institutions as centers for skepticism rather than as centers to strengthen faith. At least, that has been my personal experience, and it is also how we have arrived at the dilemma of having "unbelieving believers" and "believing unbelievers."

Essential Guide, page 98

Day **1**

CHANGING TIMES

Randy

Jesus Christ is the same yesterday and today and forever.

Hebrews 13:8

There is nothing changeable about God; we can count on Him being constant and consistent. I have seen the times we live in change, however, in response to the moving of His Holy Spirit. Where once there was rejection of the Holy Spirit's gifts, there now is acceptance. And where once there was acceptance, there is now rejection. It just goes to show that the Holy Spirit is indeed the issue of my lifetime.

It amazes me how much things change. As I tell you in today's *Essential Guide* reading, we now have unbelieving believers and believing unbelievers. Oftentimes, unbelievers have more faith for healing than believers do. How upside-down is that? It is exactly the opposite of what you would expect. How did things get into such a state?

Why is it that healing is a peripheral issue for so many Christians, when it should be central to the Gospel? And in a broader sense, why is it that so many Christians become "unbelieving believers" when it comes to the gifts of the Holy Spirit? Those are the questions we will take a look at today and in the rest of this session.

- Today's Scripture reading: Acts 19:1–6
- Today's reading from *Essential Guide*: pages 87–93

The Berean Approach

1. I quoted for you in the book the final paragraph of my seminary term paper on healing. What do you think of my statement, "The miraculous element in Christianity and the fact that God can act in this world of ours is essential to the vitality of Christianity"? (See *Essential Guide* page 88.)

   _____

   _____

   _____

2. Briefly define *unbelieving believers* and *believing unbelievers*. (See *Essential Guide* page 92.) Have you run into people in either category?

   _____

   _____

   _____

3. Name the three primary contributing causes of Christians becoming unbelieving believers. What are a few of the ways in which those causes contribute to the formation of such believers? (See *Essential Guide* page 93.)

   _____

   _____

   _____

Day 2

THE IMPACT OF EROSION

Randy

Therefore, my dear brothers and sisters, stand firm. Let nothing move you.

1 Corinthians 15:58

As we saw in Day 1 of this session, three factors contributed to the formation of what I call unbelieving believers: sociological factors, theological factors and church factors. It may seem like a highly academic exercise to you as we consider each of these factors in the days just ahead, but stay with me. The understanding you gain will help you when you actually run into unbelieving believers. You will be able to identify the thought processes behind their attitude and avoid falling into the same trap. Perhaps the Holy Spirit will even use the knowledge you gain in this session to bring light to their understanding.

We will look today at the sociological factors involved, which had a lot to do with the rise of rationalism and the humanist movement. It also did not help that as persecution ended in the Roman Empire the Church gained so many nominal members, which had a huge and long-term effect on the purity of Christianity.

We will also look at the theological factors specifically at work in the Roman Catholic Church, which ranged over hundreds of years from the influence of Augustine to that of Thomas Aquinas and beyond. When you add up all the factors, you can see the impact of erosion they had on people's beliefs in healing and the other gifts.

(In Day 3, we will move on to look at the theological factors at work in the Protestant Church, which were no less erosive.)

- Today's Scripture reading: 1 Corinthians 2:6–16
- Today's reading from *Essential Guide*: pages 94–98

The Berean Approach

1. How did the decline of persecution and the legalization of Christianity in the Roman Empire—sociological factors that seem as if they would have had a positive effect—actually dilute the purity of the Church? (See *Essential Guide* page 94.)

   _____

   _____

   _____

2. Briefly compare the warfare worldview to the blueprint worldview. (See *Essential Guide* pages 95–96.) Which viewpoint have you leaned toward, and how has it affected your attitude toward healing?

   _____

   _____

   _____

3. In what way did Jerome's translation of the word *heal* as *save* in James 5:14–15 change the Roman Catholic sacrament involving the sick? (See *Essential Guide* page 96.)

   _____

   _____

   _____

4. Have you ever had anyone tell you that their illness was the cross they carried or that their suffering glorified Jesus? Why do you suppose they believed that, and how does that take suffering out of context in light of the Bible's references to it? (See *Essential Guide* page 97.)

   _____

   _____

   _____

Day 3

NEGATIVE "ISMS"

Randy

Do not be carried away by all kinds of strange teachings.

Hebrews 13:9

Today we turn our attention to the theological factors that have resulted in the Protestant Church's rampant skepticism toward healing. That skepticism has risen out of several other "isms" that have made their way into Protestant colleges and seminaries over the years—liberalism, cessationism, dispensationalism, new liberalism and fundamentalism, with neoorthodoxy thrown in for good measure.

As you will learn in today's book reading, these "isms" have all had a negative effect on the Church and have contributed to turning many Christians into unbelieving believers. It is important to understand where these factors came from and where they took our Protestant theology surrounding the gifts of the Holy Spirit.

Again, I realize that the lessons in this session may seem academic, but you will gain much from having at least a basic understanding of where so many in the Protestant Church stand and how they got there. We will move into more practical applications of the gifts of the Spirit in the sessions ahead, and I trust you will gain some important personal experience in healing ministry. But continue in today's lesson (and in Day 4 just ahead) to lay a solid foundation for your belief in healing by learning what makes an unstable, unsuitable foundation. This knowledge will help you, and through it you can help solidify others who are questioning their beliefs.

- Today's Scripture reading: 2 Thessalonians 2:13–17
- Today's reading from *Essential Guide*: pages 98–102

The Berean Approach

1. In what way are liberal theologians and cessationists on the opposite ends of the theological spectrum from each other? (See *Essential Guide* pages 98–99.)

   _____

   _____

   _____

2. Why do you think dispensationalism's ultrapessimistic view became so prevalent, even among Pentecostals? (See *Essential Guide* page 100.)

   _____

   _____

   _____

3. What do new liberals who demythologize Scripture believe about the supernatural events that the Bible relates? (See *Essential Guide* pages 101–102.)

   _____

   _____

   _____

4. What have most denominationally trained ministers been trained in when it comes to healing, miracles and the supernatural today? (See *Essential Guide* page 102.)

   _____

   _____

   _____

5. Fundamentalists believe that rare healings can occur, but they would not attribute them to the gifts of healing. What would they attribute them to? (See *Essential Guide* page 102.)

Day 4

CHARISMATIC CLOSETS
Randy

> We are no longer to be children, tossed here and there by waves and carried about by every wind of doctrine, by the trickery of men, by craftiness in deceitful scheming; but speaking the truth in love, we are to grow up in all aspects into Him who is the head, even Christ . . .
>
> Ephesians 4:14–15 NASB

In Days 2 and 3 we looked at the sociological and theological factors that contributed to the formation of unbelieving believers. Today we will examine the Church factors in both the Roman Catholic and Protestant denominations. Both groups made decisions that have undermined people's faith for healing and miracles.

Today's reading in the book details three factors in the Roman Catholic Church and eight factors in the Protestant church that fit into this category. Something I find interesting is that one of the factors overlaps between the two groups—that of establishing "charismatic closets." Both Roman Catholic and Protestant churches have made some effort in the past to accommodate their charismatic members, but that accommodation involved segregating those who moved in the Holy Spirit's gifts into separate meetings outside of the regular services or liturgies. This quarantine was a compromise that kept the members in the churches but kept the Holy Spirit out of congregational worship. Sadly, that contained and controlled the impact of those who operated in the Spirit's gifts.

But that is just one factor among many, as you will see. Thankfully, the effects of some of these factors are declining noticeably.

We still have a long way to go, however, to get unbelieving believers to believe again in healing and the gifts.

- Today's Scripture reading: Ephesians 4:11–24
- Today's reading from *Essential Guide*: pages 103–110

The Berean Approach

1. How is Johann Blumhardt's statement, that there were many things he did not know, but the one thing he did know was that Jesus is victor, an apt statement for us all?

2. How did the quarantine measure of establishing "charismatic closets" in both Roman Catholic and Protestant churches place the workings of God through the Spirit's gifts outside the experience of most church members?

3. When it comes to the moral failure of high-visibility leaders, what must we remember regarding the Holy Spirit's confirmation? (See *Essential Guide* page 107.)

4. In the case of missionaries Dave and Diana that I told you about in the book, I mentioned that they parted ways amicably with their missionary agency, which held a cessationist viewpoint. What value might there be in parting ways amicably with those who do not hold the same viewpoint on healing ministry and the gifts of the Spirit as you do?

Session 4 Video Guide

1. We are people who believe in the _supernatural_ realm. Perhaps more today than anytime in the last _300_ years, there's been a change.

2. In Greek and in Hebrew, _wind_ is a word that can be translated "spirit."

3. Unbelieving believers are Christians who believe in Jesus as _Lord_ and _Savior_, who have committed their lives to Him and attend church on some type of a regular basis, and yet they don't believe in _healing_ or the sign gifts or _miracles_ today.

4. Believing unbelievers are people who are not committed to Jesus Christ, who have not been _Born again_, yet they believe in the _Supernatural_

5. The ideal is to have _believing believers_

6. Knowing His Word, in us, and obeying Him cause us to be able to _hear_ Him, which then cause us to have _faith_.

7. Whether you're a liberal pastor or a fundamentalist pastor, your theology as far as _today_ and expecting God to move _today_ make the fundamentalist and the liberal strange _bed fellows_

8. When Christianity became the _official_ religion of the Roman Empire, Randy said that the church was "flooded with people who were joining for the _wrong_ reasons . . . as a lot of people were added to the church without, in my opinion, being added to _Christ_."

9. Randy said, "I put it this way: Humankind was _dehuman_ by the _-ised_ humanist movement."

10. The ~~poor~~ *warfare* worldview is that God is in ~~the ?~~ blueprint of everything, and nothing happens unless He *caused* it.

11. We have *victory* over sickness, disease, demons and damnation because of this *Christus Victor* (view), and that was basically the preaching for the first *1,000* years, which accommodated this *warfare* worldview. . . .

12. Randy finished with, "Trust and believe. Be a believing believer, and be a *humble* believing believer, and build a *bridge*, not a *wall*, to those who are unbelieving believers."

HEALING AND THE KINGDOM

Bill

The Lord's return is beautiful and will be the ultimate culmination of events, but our assignment is not to go to heaven. It is to bring heaven to earth through prayer and obedience, by embracing the ministry of Jesus.

Healing was a major part of Jesus' ministry. There is no cancer in heaven. Neither is there any blindness or deafness or any other malady in that realm. Freedom from disease is God's will on earth. Period. God has not commanded us to pray for healing in order to frustrate us. Neither is prayer a spiritual exercise created to make us hungry for eternity. We are not to believe, *Physical health will never happen here; this can only happen in heaven. It is reserved as our eternal reward.* Heaven is meant to invade earth in this area.

Essential Guide, page 118

Day **1**

PARTNERSHIP RESTORED

Bill

The heavens are the heavens of the LORD, but the earth
He has given to the sons of men.

Psalm 115:16

Partnership with humanity in ruling over this planet was God's *Plan A* right from the beginning. The Fall of man derailed that plan temporarily, but God had another plan that put it back on track—His redemptive plan of sending Jesus as a man to buy back humanity and defeat the devil. Jesus modeled for us how humanity can partner with God in fulfilling His plans. He restored our partnership with the Father.

God's plans are stunning, not to mention surprising. That He would partner with us at all, that He would delight in delegating responsibility for the earth to us, is amazing. But as you will see in today's reading (and in Day 2's), to carry out God's plans for this planet, we need to start with prayer. God's will is for us to pray His will. That kind of prayer connects our heart with His and releases His purposes into the earth.

- Today's Scripture reading: Luke 4:1–8; Matthew 28:16–20
- Today's reading from *Essential Guide*: pages 111–116

The Berean Approach

1. What was God's simple assignment for those He created in His image? (See Genesis 1:28 and *Essential Guide* page 111.)

   _____

   _____

   _____

2. For us to have true dominion over this world, what must we conform our thought life to, and what attitudes or mindsets must we carry? (See *Essential Guide* page 114.)

   _____

   _____

   _____

3. Why is it a faulty assumption to think that if something is God's will, it will automatically be done? (See *Essential Guide* page 115.)

   _____

   _____

   _____

Day 2

INVADING THE EARTH

Bill

Your kingdom come. Your will be done, on earth as it is
in heaven.

Matthew 6:10

We are heaven's invasion force. Our task is to invade the earth and establish in it the culture of the empire of heaven. As I tell you in today's book reading, that is the very essence of the word *apostle*. We are accustomed to thinking of that word in relation to Christianity, but it did not originate in the early Church. It was a secular term that described the mindset of someone who was carrying out a very specific mandate. An *apostle* was the leader of a special envoy sent to invade a culture and completely transform the daily lives of its citizens.

If that is not a description of what the Kingdom of God is meant to do on the earth, I don't know what is. That is why the Lord's Prayer is such an apostolic prayer. It clearly expresses the mandate of the Church to transform the culture of earth until it reflects the culture of heaven. "On earth as it is in heaven" is both our prayer and our mandate.

That prayer and mandate include healing and deliverance. After all, wholeness and freedom are part of heaven's culture. They need to be part of ours.

- Today's Scripture reading: Isaiah 9:6–7; Matthew 10:1–8; 2 Corinthians 4:1–6
- Today's reading from *Essential Guide*: pages 116–118

The Berean Approach

1. What two basic parts does the Lord's Prayer contain, and what does the second part focus on? (See *Essential Guide* page 116.)

2. In what way is the Lord's Prayer an apostolic prayer? (See *Essential Guide* pages 117–118.)

3. In light of our apostolic mandate, what does it mean to say that the more the Church realizes who she is, the less she wants to be rescued?

4. How is heaven invading earth both simple and complex? (See *Essential Guide* page 118.)

Day **3**

A FULLER SALVATION

Bill

Jesus was going through all the cities and villages, teaching in their synagogues and proclaiming the gospel of the kingdom, and healing every kind of disease and every kind of sickness.

Matthew 9:35

How can salvation get any fuller than being saved? Today, the majority of Christians would say that it cannot. I would not be among them. Somewhere between the time Jesus came to save, heal and deliver and the present day we live in, we narrowed the meaning of the word *salvation* to "the forgiveness of sin." As a whole, it is easy for us to have faith for that. When we see people get saved, we rejoice that their sins have been forgiven and that they are on their way to heaven. And I would never diminish the importance of that transformation.

But do we have faith for their healing? Jesus made provision to save the whole person—spirit, soul and body. *Sozo*, the original Greek word for "save," carries all of that in its meaning, so it is entirely reasonable to expect to see healing and deliverance accompany salvation.

Our expectations, however, are unreasonable, and by that I mean they are now too low. Rather than having faith for partial salvation, we need to have faith for a fuller salvation. That is the topic of today's lesson.

- Today's Scripture reading: Acts 3:1–10
- Today's reading from *Essential Guide*: pages 118–122

The Berean Approach

1. Whenever Jesus proclaimed His message, what followed and why? (See *Essential Guide* page 119.)

   _____

   _____

   _____

2. Although forgiveness of sin is the ultimate miracle, what more did God intend in the message of salvation? (See *Essential Guide* pages 119–120.)

   _____

   _____

   _____

3. Why do you think we often have more faith for someone's conversion than we do for his or her healing?

   _____

   _____

   _____

4. In what way have you experienced the truth that pursuing the impossible is our nature in Christ?

   _____

   _____

   _____

Day **4**

CHANGING OUR PERSPECTIVE

Bill

God anointed Jesus of Nazareth with the Holy Spirit and
with power, who went about doing good and healing all
who were oppressed by the devil, for God was with Him.

Acts 10:38 NKJV

We cannot be afraid to pursue more and take risks. We
cannot create our theology around what does not happen. We cannot settle at a comfortable level. We cannot
maintain that God sends sickness, when in fact it is the devil who
comes to steal, kill and destroy. We cannot have the Spirit of the res-
urrected Christ living in us and turn our backs on the cry of the sick.

That is quite a list of "cannots," and yet many of us do them.
Many Christians do one or more of all those things, when what they
need is a change in their perspective.

How do we change our perspective so that we reflect Jesus, who
Himself reflected perfect theology? Repentance. Sorrow over the
sin of misrepresenting God to others. When we repent, we change
direction. We change perspective. We renew our minds and revitalize
our reflection of the One who came to save, heal and deliver.

- Today's Scripture reading: Philippians 2:5–11
- Today's reading from *Essential Guide*: pages 122–127

The Berean Approach

1. In what way have we made the Gospel a message solely about what we will have access to after we die? How has this contributed to forming what my co-author, Randy, calls unbelieving believers?

   _____

   _____

   _____

2. Why do you think joy has such a healing effect? (See *Essential Guide* pages 124–125.) How have you experienced this for yourself?

   _____

   _____

   _____

3. Even though Jesus is eternally God, when He came to earth He chose to live among us within the restrictions of a man who had no sin and was empowered by the Holy Spirit. Why was that so important for us? (See *Essential Guide* page 125.)

   _____

   _____

   _____

4. In regard to sickness, what does it mean to say that somewhere in today's faulty theology, God took over the devil's job? (See *Essential Guide* page 126.) How has this influenced the Church in regard to healing?

   _____

   _____

   _____

5. How does knowing that Jesus brought His world with Him change the way we think?

   _____

   _____

   _____

Session 5 Video Guide

1. God created us to _____ Him and to _____ His glorious rule—His goodness, His kindness—all over the earth, and in the process _____ every obstacle.

2. "On earth as it is in heaven" is an _____ prayer.

3. In the Lord's Prayer, Jesus sets the mandate, the focus, the _____ for prayer, and then He _____ it.

4. When we talk about the _____, we're not talking about a bureaucracy, we're not talking about church _____, we're not talking about any of those things. We're talking about _____.

5. The Kingdom is a _____ group of people who get to experience and release the _____ of God in a very _____ way.

6. The will of God in essence is God wants it _____ like it is _____.

7. Let God's goodness _____ your _____.

8. It's _____ theology to look at a loss or a problem and say, "Well, God just _____ it to be so."

9. You can't use the Old Testament to _____ Jesus; you have to use Jesus to _____ the Old Testament.

10. You can give what you _____. If you will _____ for that place of peace and breakthrough personally, it will _____ you to influence your surroundings.

11. Sickness is to my _____ what sin is to my _____, and salvation deals with the whole _____.

12. _____ is the answer to the sin problem. _____ is the answer to the torment problem. _____ is the answer to the disease problem.

HEALING AND THE AUTHORITY OF THE BELIEVER

Bill

Authority is quite different than power. Power is explosive and environmental in the sense that it is the actual atmosphere of heaven that changes the atmosphere of earth. Authority is a position given by Jesus Himself. A policeman carries a gun (power), but he also carries a badge (authority). The badge does much more than the gun.

Power is the atmosphere of heaven. Ministering in power is like catching a wave. Authority is like starting a wave. Things start happening because of who God says we are and what our responsibilities are. Faith is what connects us to this realm of authority—we have to believe what He says about us and what He has commissioned us to do.

Essential Guide, pages 137–138

Day **1**

REVEL IN THE REWARDS

Bill

Jesus said to them, "My food is to do the will of Him who sent Me and to accomplish His work."

John 4:34

There is a price to pay in following God's lead. There is opposition. There is conflict. There is sacrifice. But all that is nothing compared to the rewards we reap. We need to remember that it is in God's nature to be a Rewarder of those who seek Him, as Hebrews 11:6 says.

The joy of obedience far outstrips the pain. Jesus paid the ultimate price to do the will of the Father, but reaped the redemption of the whole human race. He endured the cross for the *joy* set before Him (see Hebrews 12:2).

I think that as believers, many of us need to stop reveling in the pain of obedience and start reveling in the rewards instead. I have found that it is sheer joy to follow God's lead, even though it costs something along the way. (The reward of heaven far outweighs any cost.) Some special moments in healing ministry have come my way because I was willing to follow His lead into some exciting experiences. I tell you about one of those in today's *Essential Guide* pages.

- Today's Scripture reading: Hebrews 12:1–11
- Today's reading from *Essential Guide*: pages 129–132

The Berean Approach

1. What does it mean to say that sometimes what we love is measured by what we hate?

   _____

   _____

   _____

2. What happens when we emphasize the price we pay to obey above the rewards that obedience brings? (See *Essential Guide* page 130.)

   _____

   _____

   _____

3. What is your default approach to praying for the sick? Has God ever had you set it aside to make room for something He wanted to do in a different way? (If you do not have a default approach, Randy's Five-Step Prayer Model that we cover in Session 11 is a great one to adopt.)

   _____

   _____

   _____

4. In what way is begging God to heal someone an assumption that we have more mercy than He does? Why do you think we tend to pray for what we already possess?

   _____

   _____

   _____

Day 2

CAUSE AND EFFECT

Bill

The kingdom of God is not a matter of talk but of power.

1 Corinthians 4:20 NIV

Faith comes by hearing. Breakthrough comes by recognizing a gift of faith operating in a person. Transformation comes by carrying His presence. All cause and effect.

Jesus healed all who came because God was with Him. Again, cause and effect. And the anointing that qualified Him qualifies you and me.

That thought should give us the boldness we need to become *believing* believers. Filled with the power of God, we can boldly declare the Gospel and expect to see signs and wonders confirm it. It is His presence and power that changes the world around us. As I said in Day 1, it is just a matter of following His lead. With God, facing the most impossible of assignments becomes entirely possible.

- Today's Scripture reading: John 5:17–24
- Today's reading from *Essential Guide*: pages 132–136

The Berean Approach

1. In what way can past success prevent us from greater ministry? (See *Essential Guide* page 133.)

---

2. Describe a time when you recognized what God was doing by watching how someone else was responding to the Holy Spirit.

---

3. What kind of fruit comes out of being a *believing* believer? (See *Essential Guide* page 135.)

---

4. What is it that often attracts the miracle into a given situation? Why? (See *Essential Guide* page 135.)

Day **3**

RIDING THE WAVES

Bill

And the power of the Lord was present for Him to perform healing.

Luke 5:17

If you have ever gone surfing, you will understand the comparisons I make in today's *Essential Guide* reading. To catch a wave, surfers position themselves in the water, watch what the waves are doing and paddle like crazy to catch a good one. Riding the manifestation of God's power is no different, and it is fully as exciting. When the atmosphere of heaven rolls in and changes the atmosphere of earth, it can be a wild and wonderful ride.

Catching the waves is not all there is to it, though. Sometimes we have to do more than sit back and watch. We have to *start* a wave, which is something we can do in the spiritual that surfers obviously cannot do in the natural. (Though many wish they could!) Using the authority Jesus gave us is like starting a wave, and that is a whole different thing than simply catching one. But the two go together—ministering in power and ministering in authority—which is what I talk about more in the book pages you are about to read.

- Today's Scripture reading: Matthew 14:22–31
- Today's reading from *Essential Guide*: pages 136–139

The Berean Approach

1. Why do you think Jesus specifically gave His disciples both power and authority? (See *Essential Guide* page 136.)

_____

_____

_____

2. How do authority and power differ in the spiritual sense? (See *Essential Guide* page 137.)

_____

_____

_____

3. Why do things start happening when we use our authority in Christ? What connects us to this realm of authority? (See *Essential Guide* page 138.)

_____

_____

_____

Day 4

AN UPGRADED
ASSIGNMENT

Bill

So Jesus said to them again, "Peace be with you; as the
Father has sent Me, I also send you."

John 20:21

It is one thing to operate under the umbrella of someone else's
anointing, as I did in today's story in *Essential Guide* about how I
ministered with my friend Dick in his gift. Likewise, the disciples
functioned under Jesus' anointing for the three and a half years that
He was with them. Such times are exciting and instructional for us.

It is quite another thing, however, to receive an upgraded assignment from God that puts us on the front lines of ministry, function-
ing ourselves in power and authority from on high. For that, we
need our own experience with God. We need to ready ourselves to
walk in the authority Jesus gave us, and we need to wait until we
are clothed with that same power from on high that the disciples
waited on before leaving Jerusalem after the resurrection.

That personal experience with the Holy Spirit is what equips and
empowers us to carry out our upgraded assignment successfully.
Don't leave home without it.

- Today's Scripture reading: Luke 3:21–22; John 1:19–34
- Today's reading from *Essential Guide*: pages 139–141

The Berean Approach

1. After Jesus' resurrection, in what way were the disciples called to accelerate what they had already been doing? (See *Essential Guide* page 141.)

2. What two things did the disciples need in order to carry out their upgraded assignment? (See *Essential Guide* page 141.)

3. Besides an understanding of the authority we have in Christ, what else do we need to have before leaving our ministry base?

Session 6 Video Guide

1. The _____ mind comes out of _____ and _____ with the Lord.

2. _____ is the manifestation of Presence; _____ is the manifestation of identity.

3. We're always trying to _____ the _____ of what God is doing, and operating in _____ is that.

4. The _____ between power and authority is this: In power, you _____ a wave. In authority, you _____ the wave.

5. Authority comes in the _____; power comes in the _____.

6. Bill said about being refilled by the Holy Spirit, "My vessel is _____, I _____, and I need to be _____ over and over and over again."

7. The _____ to heal the sick is a _____ from God, so anytime He uses any of us in that way, it always goes back to His _____ operating in us.

8. When you lay hands on someone and _____ heals them through you, you're delivering a _____ that someone else _____.

9. If Jesus only did what the _____ did and everyone He ministered to was healed, then maybe there's a _____!

10. The Holy Spirit knows what He's doing, and He wants to _____ us, and He has a _____ for everyone to be well.

CREATING
A FAITH CULTURE

Bill

The best way to create an atmosphere of faith is to start with an overwhelming awareness of need and realize the impossibility of our assignment from God. Often we get caught up with what is possible through human effort. We build our buildings and pay for great programs. While those things are good, it is tragic when they become the high point of our celebration of Christian achievement. When that is the case, it makes us no different than one of the many good service clubs in our communities. We are responsible for more. We are responsible to live in such a way that the Gospel that Jesus lived, preached and demonstrated will once again take center stage in world affairs. The impossible invites the faith-*full* to come and conquer.

Essential Guide, page 146

Day **1**

AN APPETITE
FOR THE IMPOSSIBLE

Bill

Jesus said to them, "With people this is impossible, but with God all things are possible."

Matthew 19:26

Do you have an appetite for the impossible? While it is normal for every believer to have faith, an appetite for the impossible is not automatic. That is why the *Essential Guide* chapter you are reading throughout this session is important. When you create a faith culture, it increases people's appetite for the impossible.

Every born-again believer has the DNA of Christ, and during Jesus' time on earth He certainly never backed down from accomplishing the impossible. If we are to represent Him accurately to the world, should we back down? Yet as I tell you in today's book reading, sometimes disappointment or bad teaching can make us lose our appetite, so to speak. Many of us need to deal with those two roadblocks that stand in the way of pursuing the miraculous, and this session will help. It is also a matter of realizing how born-again we actually are. With Christ's DNA in us, nothing is impossible.

- Today's Scripture reading: 1 Corinthians 2
- Today's reading from *Essential Guide*: pages 145–149

The Berean Approach

1. What kind of domino effect do you think one city that belongs entirely to God might have on a nation?

   _____

   _____

   _____

2. What is the best way to create an atmosphere of faith, and why? (See *Essential Guide* page 146.)

   _____

   _____

   _____

3. How do you think stopping for the one, as Heidi Baker puts it, sets us up for the transformation of cities and nations?

   _____

   _____

   _____

4. In what way does unresolved disappointment deaden a person's heart to a desire for the impossible? (See *Essential Guide* page 148. In Day 4 of this session, we will look at steps toward healing such disappointment.)

   _____

   _____

   _____

5. What do we need to remember if we pray for someone and the person does not get healed? (See *Essential Guide* pages 148–149.)

   _____

   _____

   _____

Day 2

CONTINUOUS PURSUIT

Bill

And without faith it is impossible to please Him, for he who comes to God must believe that He is and that He is a rewarder of those who seek Him.

Hebrews 11:6

Belief in the miraculous is one thing; pursuit is another. I pursue the things I want to see happen in the spiritual rather than sitting back and waiting for them to come to me. My pursuit is based on my faith that God is indeed a Rewarder of those who seek Him. I desire to live out that revelation.

In today's reading from *Essential Guide*, I list for you seven things I do to increase my personal experience in faith and the experience of the church I pastor. The list includes specifically and passionately crying out to God, studying the Bible to look for models to follow of those who moved in the Spirit, researching the history of some of the great generals of God's army, pursuing impartation from those who live a miraculous lifestyle, associating with those who are giant killers, living a life of risk and radical obedience, and correctly stewarding what God has given.

I detail each of these things a little more for you in the book pages you are about to read. Adopt them as part of your continuous pursuit, if you have not already done so, and see what happens. For me, they have become key elements in building a culture of faith personally and congregationally.

- Today's Scripture reading: Mark 9:14–29; Jude 20
- Today's reading from *Essential Guide*: pages 149–152

The Berean Approach

1. Can we assume that miracle breakthroughs will simply function in our lives without passionate prayer? Why not? (See *Essential Guide* pages 149–150.)

2. What does it mean to eat the meat and throw out the bones in regard to studying people whose stories did not end well? (See *Essential Guide* page 151.)

3. Have you ever hung around a giant killer and had some of his or her qualities rub off on you? How did that affect your faith?

4. Why is correctly stewarding what God has given us the way that we obtain more? (See *Essential Guide* page 152.)

5. Of the seven things on my list, which one has affected your personal experience of faith the most? Which one do you most need to adopt?

Day **3**

LIVING WITH
THE UNEXPLAINABLE

Bill

And we know that God causes all things to work together
for good to those who love God, to those who are called
according to His purpose.

Romans 8:28

I say it in today's book reading, but let me also say it here: *The goodness of God is the cornerstone of our theology.* When we understand God's goodness, hope rises in our hearts. When we know that He is for us, we can live at peace with the unexplainable. We can know that He has not failed us, whatever the circumstances.

It helps to realize that not everything works out perfectly the first time. We are still in process, particularly when it comes to seeing the miraculous. In the book pages you are about to read, I give the example of praying for a family member without seeing healing as a result. Many of us have had that experience, which can usher in such disappointment in response (along with some questionable theology). It is a difficult area that can put obstacles in the way of pursuing future healings.

Dealing with disappointment is inevitable, however, when you are dealing with the miraculous lifestyle. To get past disappointment, the thing to do is to give up your right to understand, along with giving up any false notion that tragedy is attributable to God. Jesus healed *all* who came to Him. He raised people from the dead, because not everyone dies in God's timing. Whatever results we have seen—or have not seen—in healing ministry in the past, the standard Jesus set is the only one worth aiming for.

- Today's Scripture reading: Mark 6:1–6; Luke 4:14–22
- Today's reading from *Essential Guide*: pages 152–156

The Berean Approach

1. In what way is repentance a good place to start in expanding your Kingdom experience? (See *Essential Guide* page 153.)

   _____

   _____

   _____

2. Why is it vitally important to avoid creating a foolish doctrine or belief in order to take away the pressure of mystery or of the unexplainable? (See *Essential Guide* page 154.)

   _____

   _____

   _____

3. Why do you think that learning to live with the unexplainable is one of the most necessary ingredients of the Christian life?

   _____

   _____

   _____

4. Think of a situation in which you have had to do battle with the giant of disappointment. How did God's touch redeem the situation for you? (If you are still in that battle, Day 4's lesson just ahead will help you.)

   _____

   _____

   _____

Day 4

THANKFUL AND HUNGRY

Bill

Therefore let us draw near with confidence to the throne of grace, so that we may receive mercy and find grace to help in time of need.

Hebrews 4:16

We talked a little in Day 3 about how disappointment can be a huge obstacle to living the miracle lifestyle. It can weaken your spiritual immune system, but you do not have to leave it festering in your heart. Today's reading in the book equips you with some tools you can use to enable yourself to heal from disappointment. As you employ each of these tools, you take a step toward pursuing the miraculous again.

In today's reading, I cover four important tools or steps you can take toward overcoming disappointment. Being honest with God and baring your soul is the first. Listening to Him closely is the second. I like to turn to the book of Psalms in this second step and read until I hear my voice and see my heart's cry expressed there. Then healing comes as I meditate on His Word. The third step is to receive peace. Keep going before God until His peace starts to invade you, and don't forget what I mentioned about that in Day 3: Giving up your right to understand the unexplainable opens the door for the peace that passes all understanding. Finally, the fourth step is to feed your heart correctly. It is all about the power of the testimony. What a powerful tool! (In fact, it is so powerful that it is the whole focus of Session 8.) When you focus on what God has done rather than what He does not seem to be doing, it builds faith and blocks the spirit of offense.

The right attitude is also an absolute necessity when you are healing from disappointment. Being thankful for all God has already done and staying hungry for the more He has promised will take you places you could never go with a wrong attitude about past disappointments. If you want to stay spiritually healthy and experience more of what God has for you, you need to stay thankful and hungry.

- Today's Scripture reading: Matthew 11:2–15
- Today's reading from *Essential Guide*: pages 156–160

The Berean Approach

1. What is the difference between baring your soul before God and accusing Him in the name of honesty?

   _____

   _____

   _____

2. I mention in the book that in taking care of the issues of the heart, Proverbs 4:23 has become a priority verse for me over the last forty years. Which verse or verses have become a priority for you as you work to keep your heart clean and devoted to God?

   _____

   _____

   _____

3. Dwelling on what God is not doing (or does not seem to be doing) ultimately leads to questioning His nature as good. What does it mean to live life by feeding on His faithfulness instead? (See *Essential Guide* page 159.)

   _____

   _____

   _____

4. What are the two main attitudes we must cultivate as we pursue the miracle lifestyle Jesus assigned to us? (See *Essential Guide* page 160.) How are you doing with your cultivation of those?

_____

_____

_____

Session 7 Video Guide

1. Faith has _____ in God's nature; He is the _____.

2. Faith is not the result of _____; it's the result of _____.

3. Faith is not _____ to intellect; it's just _____.

4. Faith doesn't deny the _____ of a problem. Faith denies the problem a place of _____.

5. Faith is the _____ of encountering the _____ _____.

6. It's _____ that in disappointment, we learn how to be _____ with God.

7. To have the _____ that passes understanding, you have to give up your right to _____.

8. The _____ way to discouragement is focusing on what God "_____ _____."

9. To be _____ people, we have to know how to give thanks in spite of what we don't yet _____, to give Him praise in the middle of _____ circumstances.

10. _____ is probably one of the most _____ influences in our lives.

11. What happens when you give thanks for that which is _____? It becomes _____.

THE POWER
OF THE TESTIMONY

Bill

The *testimony of Jesus* is a spoken or written record of anything Jesus has done. And the testimony of Jesus is the spirit of prophecy. Any time we share something that God has done in our lives, we release the spirit of prophecy. *Prophecy* comes in two main forms, one to foretell the future, and the other to release a word that changes the present. I believe the testimony of Jesus releases a prophetic anointing that has an effect on present realities. Things become possible in the present that were not available until the testimony was given. It is as though the testimony reveals what God wants to "do again."

Essential Guide, page 163

Day **1**

A LEGAL PRECEDENT FOR MIRACLES

Bill

For the testimony of Jesus is the spirit of prophecy.

Revelation 19:10

Testimonies are exciting, but giving a testimony goes far beyond telling a good story. Certainly testimonies build faith, encourage us and witness to the goodness of God, but they go beyond even that. They actually set a legal precedent for the miraculous. In today's reading you will see what I mean by that, and it will increase your appreciation for the testimonies you hear about the things God has done.

The word *testimony* itself has an amazing origin. Coming from a word that means "do again," a testimony reveals what God wants to do again. What He does for one person, He wants to do again for others, and for you and me.

As you will see in my stories today about leg muscles being healed and other healings, one testimony about a miracle can have a snowball effect. God repeats miracle after miracle as a result. Testimonies carry a prophetic anointing that affects our present reality. They help move us forward into the miraculous.

- Today's Scripture reading: Acts 10:34–43
- Today's reading from *Essential Guide*: pages 161–166

The Berean Approach

1. Anytime we share something that God has done in our lives, what is released and what does it affect? (See *Essential Guide* page 163.)

   _____

   _____

   _____

2. Why do you think it is that when a testimony is given, things become possible in the present that were not available until the testimony was given?

   _____

   _____

   _____

3. In what way do testimonies reveal God's heart and set a legal precedent for miracles? (See *Essential Guide* page 163.)

   _____

   _____

   _____

4. Briefly describe a time when you witnessed a snowball effect in response to a testimony. (If you have not yet seen that effect, be on the lookout for it as you go through the remainder of this study.)

   _____

   _____

   _____

Day 2

KEEPING THE TESTIMONY
IS KEY

Bill

You should diligently keep the commandments of the Lord your God, and His testimonies and His statutes which He has commanded you.

Deuteronomy 6:17

I know today's reading in the book is one of the shortest in this study, but it contains one of the key principles of Scripture: *the importance of keeping the testimony.* If we can get this key principle down in our Christian lives, it can change everything. Remember, we talked yesterday about how the anointing on a testimony can change present reality.

Testimonies are a priceless gift and treasure because they reveal God's nature and His heart. In the same way that we keep—watch, preserve, observe and protect—God's commandments, we also need to keep His testimonies.

You hear a lot of talk in the Church about the importance of keeping God's commandments, and that is right and good. But you don't often hear much about keeping the testimony. One of my goals in this session is to change that.

- Today's Scripture reading: Deuteronomy 6
- Today's reading from *Essential Guide*: pages 166–167

The Berean Approach

1. Commandments show us how to live, and statutes show us how to think. What do testimonies show us? (See *Essential Guide* page 166.)

   _____

   _____

   _____

2. How do you think developing the practice of keeping the testimony might also help in developing a spiritually healthy culture that contains the ability to sustain a great move of God? (See *Essential Guide* page 167.)

   _____

   _____

   _____

3. I tell you in yesterday and today's book pages how we have incorporated keeping the testimony into our church life, our staff and even our board meetings. What practices in your personal life and corporate church life help you keep God's testimonies? (If nothing comes to mind, start thinking about what you can do to change that.)

   _____

   _____

   _____

Day 3

USHERING IN THE
MERCY SEAT

Bill

You shall put the mercy seat on top of the ark, and in the
ark you shall put the testimony which I will give to you.

Exodus 25:21

As I said in Day 1 of this session, testimonies involve far
more than the telling of a good story. When you share a
testimony, you are giving your listeners an invitation to taste
of God's mercy for themselves. You are ushering the mercy seat of
God into their lives.

Did you know that the Ark of the Covenant in the Old Testament,
on top of which sat the mercy seat, was also called the Ark of the
Testimony? There is a reason for that, and I explain more about it
in today's book pages.

Forgetting God's testimony is like forgetting God's mercy. And
when we forget His mercy, we forget the miraculous. We stop looking for it, and things go downhill from there. The children of Israel
made that mistake a time or two in their history, as have many of
us today. But when we are careful to keep the testimony instead,
it acts like a lens through which we see not *what is* in our present
circumstances, but *what can be*, through the mercy and intervention
of a miraculous God.

- Today's Scripture reading: Psalm 78
- Today's reading from *Essential Guide*: pages 167–170

The Berean Approach

1. Why is it that keeping the testimony has a direct effect on the life of obedience? (See *Essential Guide* page 168.)

   _____

   _____

   _____

2. What is it about seeing the Lord's miraculous ways that raises our confidence level as Christians? How does that make keeping the testimony all the more important?

   _____

   _____

   _____

3. What are some of the ways in which we can sustain our supernatural way of thinking? (See *Essential Guide* page 169.)

   _____

   _____

   _____

4. What does it mean to say that sharing a testimony is like inviting the uninitiated into a relationship with God and His mercy? (See *Essential Guide* page 170.)

   _____

   _____

   _____

CHANGE
IN THE ATMOSPHERE
Bill

Tell of His glory among the nations, His wonderful deeds
among all the peoples.

Psalm 96:3

Atmospheric conditions are even more important in the spiritual than they are in the natural. A change in the spiritual atmosphere can change everything. Testimonies bring about that kind of change in the atmosphere.

I tell you in today's book reading that I don't want to live in reaction to the devil; I want to live in response to the Lord. Our ability to do that has a lot to do with whether or not we keep the testimony. It is all about what we choose to focus on, because what we focus on sets the atmosphere around us.

When I visit a city or nation where the Christian leaders are more focused on the area's strongholds than they are on keeping the testimony of God's miraculous works there, I know they need a change in the atmosphere. That is where testimonies come in. People need to arm themselves with testimonies that counteract an area's widespread hopelessness with stories of God's intervention and healing. Spreading such testimonies spreads hope and increases people's expectations of what God can do.

- Today's Scripture reading: Psalm 96:1–8
- Today's reading from *Essential Guide*: pages 171–172

The Berean Approach

1. I never want to set my spiritual agenda because I am influenced by or impressed with the devil's success. How can we avoid doing that? (See *Essential Guide* page 171.)

   _____

   _____

   _____

2. What can happen when testimonies spread throughout a city that has been under a particular stronghold of the enemy? (See *Essential Guide* pages 171–172.)

   _____

   _____

   _____

3. When you focus on an area that you want to see changed through the testimony, the enemy will target that area even more. How can you turn the tide so that heaven invades earth in that area? (See *Essential Guide* page 172.)

   _____

   _____

   _____

Session 8 Video Guide

1. The _____ of Jesus is the spirit of _____ (Revelation 19:10).

2. Prophecy _____ the future or _____ the present.

3. Testimony is the revelation of God's _____ in His interactions with _____.

4. We _____ one another's testimonies.

5. If I don't have a story (testimony) that fits, I can _____ one, because they've all been _____ to me.

6. *Testimony* means "_____ _____."

7. Bill said that the very nature of God, written into the testimony, was, "When we tell the _____, it is His _____ to do it again."

8. I am _____ for the miracle I need. The _____ of Jesus qualified me.

9. The _____ can bring healing to _____.

10. You want to recognize the _____ of the Spirit because He talks differently, and sometimes He talks through _____ _____ that are set up by Him.

11. Learn to recognize what He's breathing on, because you'll tell stories not to _____ people; you'll tell stories to _____ God's nature.

HEALING AND A PROSPEROUS SOUL

Bill

God's intended realm of health is more than being able to get healed. It involves a realm of mental and emotional health that was seen clearly in the person of Jesus. He lived without regret, hatred, selfish ambition, greed, unforgiveness, anxiety, shame or guilt. He lived with the ability to bring a heavenly answer to every earthly problem. He spoke, changing the atmosphere and reality that surrounded the hearer. His miracles spoke of His nature and His intentions for the earth. He is still the Creator, carrying the perfect sense of purpose for every situation, knowing that heaven indeed must come to earth. He brokered another realm, another world into this one. He provided an example that went beyond avoiding sin. He revealed purpose and destiny. He revealed the unlimited resources available to anyone who would embrace this assignment. Jesus alone illustrated life in the black as His great purpose was to reveal the Father, the source of all these things.

Essential Guide, pages 181–182

Day 1

THE HEALTH CONNECTION

Bill

And the ransomed of the LORD will return . . . they will
find gladness and joy, and sorrow and sighing will flee away.

Isaiah 35:10

Experiencing divine healing is amazing, but simply living in
divine health is even better. God's mercy is there for us when
we need divine healing, but His heart is for us to live in divine
health—to get healthy and stay healthy—spirit, soul and body.

How do we get healthy and stay that way? First, we have to acknowledge that our condition, not just on the inside but also on
the outside, has everything to do with whether we are living with
the mind of Christ. In today's reading I talk about how medical
doctors and psychologists now acknowledge that there is a definite
connection between being healthy on the inside and enjoying good
physical health. When we have the mind of Christ within us and are
living as the ransomed of the Lord, it promotes our physical health
just as much as it does our spiritual and mental health.

On the other hand, when we are living a thought life inconsistent
with the mind of Christ—a thought life filled with things like anxiety, anger, unforgiveness and jealousy—it promotes poor physical
health. There is no doubt about it; sin weakens our immune system.
In more ways than one, "the wages of sin is death" (Romans 6:23).
But no part of that is in God's plan for His people.

- Today's Scripture reading: Psalm 31:7–12; Isaiah 35
- Today's reading from *Essential Guide*: pages 173–176

The Berean Approach

1. What happens when people's creative energies are redirected into the management of unhealthy thoughts or emotions? (See *Essential Guide* page 175.)

   _____

   _____

   _____

2. Have you ever struggled with being in the condition question 1 describes? What did you do about it? More importantly, what did God do about it when you surrendered it to Him?

   _____

   _____

   _____

3. What (in my opinion) is the greatest cause of affliction for believers? (See *Essential Guide* page 175.) What signs do you think the human body gives a person who is afflicted in this way?

   _____

   _____

   _____

4. What alternative has God given us to living with internal issues that promote poor health? (See *Essential Guide* page 176.)

   _____

   _____

   _____

Day 2

THE BEST MEDICINE

Bill

Beloved, I pray that in all respects you may prosper and be in good health, just as your soul prospers.

3 John 2

We just talked in Day 1 about how having the mind of Christ has a huge effect on our physical health. Having His mind is the best medicine possible for us—spirit, soul and body. That is because when our will reflects His, everything that has been out of place in our lives comes into alignment. But we have to cooperate with God by directing our thought life to reflect His will.

I tell the story in today's reading of a young lady with Crohn's disease whose health was more affected by what was going on in her mind than by the disease itself. Her mind was full of self-condemnation, but there is no condemnation for those who are in Christ Jesus. When she put on the mind of Christ instead of dwelling on her self-abusive thoughts, she found the physical health and healing that was her portion.

As 3 John 2 above says, when your internal world prospers, so can your external health. Internal realities really do affect external realities, and we were created to live healthy in both realities.

- Today's Scripture reading: Matthew 11:28–30; Romans 8:1–11
- Today's reading from *Essential Guide*: pages 176–181

The Berean Approach

1. Why do you think that as believers, so many of us treat being critical and harsh toward ourselves as a virtue? How should we treat ourselves instead? (See *Essential Guide* page 177.)

   _____

   _____

   _____

2. After working through today's lesson, why do you agree that deep and complete confession is one of the most essential ingredients of a healthy lifestyle? (See *Essential Guide* page 178 for my comments about that.)

   _____

   _____

   _____

3. In what way is sickness to the body like sin is to the soul? How are they dealt with similarly in Scripture? (See *Essential Guide* pages 180–181.)

   _____

   _____

   _____

Day 3

LIVING IN THE BLACK

Bill

Behold, I will bring to it [Jerusalem] health and healing, and I will heal them; and I will reveal to them an abundance of peace and truth.

Jeremiah 33:6

You would know what I mean if I asked you whether you are living in the red or the black financially, but would you know what I mean if I asked you whether you are living in the red or the black spiritually? Or what about in regard to your health?

If you are living in the red physically, you will be looking for a healing, and that is good. You should seek healing. But you have to have more in your life than the absence of negative effects from sickness or sin. Once you are healed, there is a purpose for your health that goes beyond just not being sick. God has a plan for your prosperity—spirit, soul and body. It is meant to glorify Him and promote His Kingdom, as I talk about in today's reading from *Essential Guide.*

Jesus lived in the black continually. Healthy in every respect, He ministered out of His wholeness, and He knew how to bring a heavenly solution to every earthly problem out of the unlimited resources available to Him through the Father. We have those same resources available to us. Can we handle them equally well? We need to learn how to steward them well so that we, too, can minister out of wholeness and prosperity with a purpose.

- Today's Scripture reading: Jeremiah 33:1–9; Acts 16:25–34
- Today's reading from *Essential Guide*: pages 181–184

The Berean Approach

1. While it is wrong to suggest that anyone who is sick has hidden sin in his or her life, why is it equally wrong to ignore the connection between a healthy soul and physical health? (See *Essential Guide* page 182.)

   _____

   _____

   _____

2. True wealth is not measured in bank accounts, but in what? (See *Essential Guide* page 183.)

   _____

   _____

   _____

3. Why is it important that we learn to live with blessing and actually increase in spirituality at the same time? (See *Essential Guide* page 183.)

   _____

   _____

   _____

4. What is one of the greatest signs of a prosperous soul? (See *Essential Guide* page 184.) How are you doing at displaying that sign in your life?

   _____

   _____

   _____

Day **4**

KEY PRINCIPLES
TO PRACTICE

Bill

Their souls shall be like a well-watered garden.

Jeremiah 31:12 NKJV

In Days 1, 2 and 3 of this session, we talked in depth about how healing and physical health are closely related to having a prosperous soul. Today, I want to finish this session by giving you a few principles that are key to maintaining a prosperous soul. If you will put these principles into practice, your health will increase in every area.

The first principle I talk about in today's *Essential Guide* reading is to live in a place of praise. God inhabits praise, and the more that you spend time in His manifest presence, the healthier you will be. Being thankful in every situation and giving God praise will take you beyond even good health, into being *satiated* in your soul.

The next principle I cover involves biblical meditation, which is sometimes a missing tool in today's army of believers. We need to pick up this tool and use it to find the peace that comes from intimate familiarity with God's Word. His peace is so precious—nothing brings more wholeness, soundness, health and prosperity than having the peace of God within.

The final principle I mention is doing good works. Many of us are overeager to rule, when really our strong suit is serving. When God gives us favor and promotion, it is for the purpose of serving others. It is all about learning to rule with the heart of a servant and serve with the heart of a king. I believe many more people would find healing for themselves and prosperity of soul if they would just serve someone else.

Praise, biblical meditation and good works are key principles to having a happy soul, a prosperous soul. They are also key to having a healed and healthy body.

- Today's Scripture reading: John 13:3–8
- Today's reading from *Essential Guide*: pages 184–189

The Berean Approach

1. What does it mean to have a satiated soul, and what does it reflect about God? (See *Essential Guide* page 186.)

2. Do you tend to read the Scriptures more as a book to study, a contract to learn about or a love letter from God meant for you to consume passionately? How might your response to God's Word be connected to the prosperity of your soul and the health of your body?

3. What does it mean to you to rule with the heart of a servant and serve with the heart of a king?

4. Kings in God's Kingdom do not rule to build personal empires. In what way do they rule? (See *Essential Guide* pages 187–188.)

5. Why was Jesus the ultimate example of a prosperous soul?
   (See *Essential Guide* page 188.)

Session 9 Video Guide

1. A _prosperous_ soul is not necessary to be healed, but it's necessary for a healthy _lifestyle_

2. Bill said, "We always see this _____ Father responding to the condition, the _____ cry, of people; you see it *A* to *Z*—Old, New Testament—_____ the way through."

3. Prosperity is an _____ of _____.

4. God has created us to be a _____ _____ in the earth, bringing His _____ to people that are in need, people that are in crisis.

5. _intern._ health affects _phys_ health.

6. Bill said, "If there are ongoing issues, ongoing problems, be open to the Lord _____ you how to be prosperous in soul. Don't look for the _____; look for the _____."

7. Prosperity includes _____, _____ and _____.

8. The one thing greater than healing is _health_

9. _Negative thoughts_ can war against your health.

10. You _don't_ have to be in _Living_ _perfect_ health to pray for someone else.

11. _Cry out_ _____ to God in private; look for people to _serve_ in public.

12. Your _joy_ will _liberate_ the next generation (see Zechariah 10:7).

13. Prosperity of soul not only affects our health, our finances, our relationships, but it also becomes a part of an _inherit_ that we get to leave to the following _generation_

int hlth effects phys h lth

move creatively

Jeru 33:6

_3 Jn 2_

1 Cor 14:26

prosperous abundance of life

Math 11:28

WORDS OF KNOWLEDGE FOR HEALING

Randy

I first started teaching on the activation of words of knowledge not because I wanted to be faithful to Ephesians 4:11–12, "It was he who gave some to be apostles, some to be prophets, some to be evangelists, and some to be pastors and teachers, to prepare God's people for works of service, so that the body of Christ may be built up." It was also not because I was altruistic or because I was aware of a prophecy that I was to do this. No—I began out of fear of having all the pressure on me. But regardless of the reason I started, I have since found that every time I teach on this subject, the gift is activated and/or imparted to one or more persons, and they begin to move in the gift immediately following the teaching. That had happened with my son Jeremiah when I taught him about the gift, and it usually happens with at least 10 percent of a congregation when I teach.

Essential Guide, pages 193–194

Day **1**

RECOGNIZING WORDS
FOR HEALING

Randy

But the manifestation of the Spirit is given to each one for
the profit of all: for to one is given the word of wisdom
through the Spirit, to another the word of knowledge
through the same Spirit.

1 Corinthians 12:7–8 NKJV

Words of knowledge, including those that build faith for healing, come in a variety of ways. There are dreams and visions and physical manifestations and numbers and impressions and mental pictures, to name a few that we will look at in this session. Words of knowledge can even come as a combination of multiple words that come in multiple ways. But rather than letting their variety confuse you, let it excite you. Like me, the more you learn about the various ways God uses to bring words of knowledge, the more excited you will become as you see their power in creating faith, bringing healing and changing lives.

In today's *Essential Guide* reading, I want to look with you at three of the most frequent ways words of knowledge come—by feeling, by seeing and by thinking. I also tell some stories that will help you get a clearer idea of what to watch for and what to do (and not do) once you receive a word.

Knowing how to recognize words of knowledge will make you a candidate for God to use in this way. Even if you do not know what you are doing in this area right now—also just like me when I began—you can learn how to pray for the sick more effectively by being aware of and alert for words of knowledge that come for the purpose of healing.

- Today's Scripture reading: 2 Corinthians 4:1–15
- Today's reading from *Essential Guide*: pages 191–198

The Berean Approach

1. I mention in today's reading that every time I teach on the subject of words of knowledge, the gift is activated and/or imparted to at least a percentage of the hearers. If you do not operate in this gift at present, how willing are you to let God use you in this way as you learn more about it from this session?

2. As some of my stories in today's reading show, why is it important to be as specific as you can about a word of knowledge you receive, while also being careful not to interject information or interpretation that is from you rather than God?

3. In the story I tell about a young girl being healed of a rare kidney disease, my wife, DeAnne, received a word as a mental picture, but she did not know what it was that she saw. What simple step did DeAnne take (that we should all remember) to get more information? (See *Essential Guide* page 196.)

4. Name two ways that visual words might come. What is the difference between them? (See *Essential Guide* page 197.)

_____

_____

_____

Day 2

THE LEARNING PROCESS

Randy

And this I pray, that your love may abound still more and
more in knowledge and all discernment.

Philippians 1:9 NKJV

Today I want to talk about a couple more ways in which words
of knowledge come, specifically dreams and unusual experiences. Dreams are fairly straightforward, though no less
amazing than other ways. You dream something while you sleep,
and in your waking hours it remains vivid. Then you come across
a situation that reveals it was a word from God. Then you have to
act on it and pray for the person involved. I give you a few illustrative examples of words that came as dreams in the *Essential Guide*
reading for today.

Unusual experiences are a little more complex, and it is harder
to teach about them because God can use almost anything to give
someone a word. The key is to recognize it when the Lord prompts
you, as my wife did in the story I relate in the book. Some of that
recognition comes with time and experience. As you receive more
words of knowledge, you will become more sensitive to words coming in various ways, and your confidence will increase.

Over time, you will also grow in discernment when it comes to
interpreting the words you receive. That is the other thing I want
to talk about today. As your discernment develops, it is all right to
preface the words you give with statements such as, "I think this

might have happened this way . . ." or, "I am not sure if this word is for one person or more than one. . . ."

While being as specific as possible builds people's faith, we talked in Day 1 about how misinterpretation can get in the way of someone coming forward for healing. No doubt you will experience times when you are too cautious and miss it, as I have, or when you are not cautious enough and miss it, as I also have. But in healing ministry, that is part of the learning process.

- Today's Scripture reading: Philippians 1:1–11
- Today's reading from *Essential Guide*: pages 198–202

The Berean Approach

1. Scripture contains several examples of God giving people words of knowledge in their dreams. Can you name a few? Has this ever happened to you? (If not, be aware that it may happen now that you are learning more about it.)

   _____

   _____

   _____

2. Did it surprise you to read in the book that by trial and error, you can develop greater discernment in how to interpret words of knowledge? Why or why not? (See *Essential Guide* pages 200–201 for my comments about this.)

   _____

   _____

   _____

3. Handling words of knowledge well is a learning process. What did you learn in this lesson from my stories of how I missed it?

   _____

   _____

   _____

Day 3

BEING NATURAL
IN THE SUPERNATURAL

Randy

Jesus stopped and said, "Call him." So they called to the
blind man, "Cheer up! On your feet! He's calling you."

Mark 10:49

As supernatural as they are, words of knowledge are also
practical. God gives them for a specific purpose, and when
we receive them, it helps if we handle them in a practical
manner. When we deliver them and act on them by praying for
someone, it helps if we use some commonsense, down-to-earth
wisdom about it.

What do I mean by that? I explain it more fully in today's *Essential Guide* reading, but in simple terms, it helps if we are natural in
the supernatural. Becoming what I call "spooky spiritual" is more
of a distraction to what the Holy Spirit is doing than a help. Most
people will not welcome the spooky spiritual into their daily secular
lives, whereas when we learn to move in the supernatural naturally,
doors of ministry open to us in the secular arena.

In healing ministry in general, humility and honesty go a lot further than hype. We do a better job ministering when we realize it is
the word of knowledge itself that builds faith for healing, not the way
that we present it. In fact, we are better off when we simply speak
whatever the revelation is, without trying to put our interpretation
on it. Since words of knowledge can indicate many different things,

it is important to let the Holy Spirit be the interpreter as He calls people out to be healed.

- Today's Scripture reading: Mark 10:46–52
- Today's reading from *Essential Guide*: pages 202–208

The Berean Approach

1. Why do you think it is important to model the gifts of the Holy Spirit in such a way that people will take them into their secular jobs and activities? (See *Essential Guide* page 203.)

   _____

   _____

   _____

2. Through a word of knowledge, Jesus shares who and what He wants to heal. What does that do in a person who is called out in that way for healing? (See *Essential Guide* page 204.)

   _____

   _____

   _____

3. Why is it best not to encourage prophetic people to try to figure out how to interpret a word of knowledge, particularly when the word involves numbers? (See *Essential Guide* page 206.)

   _____

   _____

   _____

4. As an important aside in today's reading, I mention what I teach in regard to words of knowledge about sensitive or private areas of the body. What boundaries have you put in place in this regard, or what boundaries will you set after working through this lesson? (For my guidelines and suggestions, see *Essential Guide* pages 207–208.)

   _____

   _____

   _____

Day 4

MARKED FOR LIFE

Randy

These who have turned the world upside down have come here too.

Acts 17:6 NKJV

When God reveals someone's physical needs through a word of knowledge and brings healing, He is often marking that person for a life change. I learned that early on, when God was using words of knowledge and healings to call out and mark for life key leaders who would help us start a church. I could tell you story after story about how such words have the power to change lives, and in today's book pages I do tell you a few.

I also tell you about an early conversation I had with a Vineyard leader who revealed to me five ways that words of knowledge come. That information has proven invaluable to me, and as you read about it, I trust it will likewise prove invaluable to you. Specifically, you can feel, think, see, read and say words of knowledge, and I go into more detail about each one of those ways in *Essential Guide*.

Once you have finished today's lesson, we will have talked about several aspects of how to receive words of knowledge and how to handle them. All that information is important and will help you as you move into more healing ministry. Equally important, however, is knowing how to pray for people once you receive a word for them. That will be the subject of Session 11 just ahead, as we look at the relational Five-Step Prayer Model that I use and teach all over the world.

- Today's Scripture reading: 2 Timothy 1:6–7; 1 John 5:1–15
- Today's reading from *Essential Guide*: pages 208–212

The Berean Approach

1. Briefly tell about a time when a word of knowledge changed your life or someone else's. How did the word mark you or that person for life?

   _____

   _____

   _____

2. I told you in the book that within a few days of my conversation with the Vineyard leader about five ways words of knowledge come, I began receiving words and soon gave my first one. Have you received words in any of those five ways? Which ones? Are there others you would like to move in?

   _____

   _____

   _____

3. If you have not previously moved in words of knowledge, what do you think you can expect now that you have learned more about how this gift operates?

   _____

   _____

   _____

4. Why is it worth the risk to give a word for someone even if you miss it and learn some humility through your attempt? (See *Essential Guide* page 212.)

   _____

   _____

   _____

Session 10 Video Guide

1. If it's going to be New Testament discipleship, it can't be sufficient to say, "I ___know___ it; I can ~~recognize it~~." You don't know it until you can ___do___ it.

2. The way you get words of knowledge is that you can ___feel___ them (pain that's not your pain), you can ___see___ them (an impression), you can ~~think~~ ~~see it~~ them (like a mental picture), you can ~~see~~ ___read___ them (you see a word on somebody), or you can ___say___ them (you hear yourself say something you didn't plan to say).

3. If you don't know how to ___recognize___ them (words of knowledge), you can be having them, but not ___know___ it.

4. You want to be as ___specific___ as possible (giving words); the more specific you are, the more ___faith___ it creates. But be careful not to interject an ___interp.___ that's really not from God.

5. Randy said, "Almost now, I never try to interpret ___#s___. I just say, 'And I'm getting a number, here it is . . .' The Holy Spirit will use the same number in ___different___ ways."

6. Be ___authentic___ in how you give words of knowledge, especially when you first start. If you're not ___sure___, don't say you are.

7. If you know whom a word is for (unless the Lord tells you directly other-wise), just go to the ___person___ it's for and give it ___private___

8. Don't lean into your ___strength___ and ___lean___ all the other different ways that you can get a word of knowledge.

9. Randy challenged us to "___ask___ for words of knowledge, take ___risks___ . . . tell your ___wrong___ in your group and also your ___admit it___"

10. Two other ways you can get words of knowledge besides those five are that you can ___experience___ them and you can ___dream___ them.

THE RELATIONAL FIVE-STEP PRAYER MODEL

Randy

Again, let me state that this is not meant as a mechanical model for prayer. I do not even like the word *model*. I do not believe this is the only way to pray for healing, and at times this model cannot be used effectively, for example in large crusades. Yet it is a model built on seeing ministry as very relational and dependent on God—and it is all done "in Jesus' name."

My final word on this prayer model is that when we first heard about it in my Baptist church, the leader of the team that came to teach us said, "Don't go out and pray for a few people and come back and say, 'This doesn't work.' No! Go out and pray for two hundred people. If you do that, you will see enough people healed to hook you for life."

Essential Guide, page 240

Day **1**

GOD'S CO-WORKERS IN HEALING

Randy

For we are God's coworkers.

1 Corinthians 3:9 HCSB

Do you think of yourself as God's co-worker in healing? If you do not, or if you have not previously ministered in healing, this particular session may renew your mind in this area. It may open up to you a whole new realm of doing the works that Jesus did. In today's book pages I talk about how, as His Church here on earth, you and I are the fullness of Christ. It therefore makes sense that we would do the things He did—and healing was one of the primary things He did.

What does the formula look like to get you started doing what He did? There isn't one. Healing ministry does not involve a mechanical formula. Think of the many and varied ways Jesus used to heal the sick. In all His different approaches, however, one basic principle stood out: In every case, out of their *relationship* Jesus perceived what the Father was doing and worked with it. His healing ministry was relational, not mechanical, as He became the Father's co-worker in bringing healing.

In the same way, as we enter into relationship with Jesus and the Father through the Holy Spirit, we become God's co-workers.

Dependent on our relationship with God, we work with the Holy Spirit to minister healing to others. And although there is not a formula to apply in every case, there is a Five-Step Prayer Model I use that I learned from John Wimber. I find it very valuable in praying for the sick in a way that relates both to the person I am praying for and to God and what He is doing. I will present that model to you in the rest of this session so that you can use it, too.

- Today's Scripture reading: Mark 16:14–20; John 14:7–25
- Today's reading from *Essential Guide*: pages 213–220

The Berean Approach

1. I tell you in today's book reading about my friend Todd White, who sees a higher percentage of healings than most people I know when he prays. What did you think of his determination in praying for about seven hundred people before he saw someone healed? What kind of difference would it make if we all had that kind of determination?

   _____

   _____

   _____

2. Why is the use of the relational Five-Step Prayer Model more suited to pastoral or personal contexts than to large crowds? (See *Essential Guide* page 217.)

   _____

   _____

   _____

3. What makes Christian healing totally different from things like Reiki and Therapeutic Touch? (See *Essential Guide* page 218.)

   _____

   _____

   _____

4. Are you in the habit of using what I call Holy Spirit etiquette to thank God for His presence and power when He answers your

prayers? Why do you think this is important? (See *Essential Guide* pages 218–219.)

Day 2

TAKING THE FIRST STEPS

Randy

The prayer of a righteous person is powerful and effective.

James 5:16

Today I want to cover with you the first two steps of the Five-Step Prayer Model I use in praying for the sick. The first step, the *interview*, involves gathering information. In today's *Essential Guide* pages I give you several examples of questions you can ask a person as you look for the root cause of his or her illness and seek to build faith for healing at the same time. Establishing a connection and seeking to get to the root of things will help you minister healing more effectively. And it almost goes without saying that you are also asking the Holy Spirit for insight during the interview process.

The second step, *diagnosis and prayer selection*, is based on the information and revelation you received in the interview process. From the interview you diagnose the root cause of a person's illness and then select an approach to take in prayer. As I tell you in the book, most of the time the appropriate choice is a prayer of command directed toward the condition itself rather than toward God. Petitionary prayers toward God belong more in a worship context. We do not need to petition Him for healing since He has already made it clear that healing people is His heart. (There are some times, though, when mixing prayers of petition and command is appropriate, and I give you some examples of that in the book.)

In today's reading I list for you the most common causes of illness and how to select a prayer for each effectively. I think you will find, as I have, that when you take these first steps of going through the *interview* and then the *diagnosis and prayer selection*, it will greatly increase the percentage of healings you will see.

- Today's Scripture reading: James 5:13–18
- Today's reading from *Essential Guide*: pages 220–228

The Berean Approach

1. What are you determining, and what are you building, in the first step of the Five-Step Prayer Model, the interview? (See *Essential Guide* page 221.)

    _____

    _____

    _____

2. Why do you think it is also important to share during the interview what a person can do (and ought not do) to work with you for a better outcome? (See *Essential Guide* page 222.)

    _____

    _____

    _____

3. What is the difference between petitionary prayers and prayers of command? (See *Essential Guide* pages 222–224.) Had you given this difference much thought before working through today's lesson? How will it change your prayers for the sick?

    _____

    _____

    _____

4. Rather than asking God to heal, what is it appropriate to petition Him for privately during healing ministry? (See *Essential Guide* page 225.)

    _____

    _____

    _____

5. Why do you think dealing with psychosomatic roots is such a significant aspect of ministering healing? (See *Essential Guide* page 226 for my thoughts on that.)

_____

_____

_____

6. What are some indications that an afflicting spirit is the root cause of a person's illness? What must you do in response? (See *Essential Guide* pages 226–227.)

_____

_____

_____

Day **3**

SPEAK—DECLARE— COMMAND

Randy

Whatever city you enter, and they receive you . . . heal the sick there, and say to them, "The kingdom of God has come near to you."

Luke 10:8–9 NKJV

After you take the first two steps of the prayer model, the *interview* and *diagnosis and prayer selection*, it is time to take the third step and speak—declare—command what needs to happen. This step is called *praying for effect*. It is time to enter into prayer ministry for the person, with an expectation that healing will take place and with thanksgiving as it begins to happen (the Holy Spirit etiquette I talked about in Day 1).

Praying for effect means that you pray to get results. You are not praying to comfort or encourage the person. You are not giving advice or preaching to him or her. You are following the Holy Spirit's lead carefully and doing what He says. And you are commanding the person's body to respond, because as an ambassador of the Kingdom of God you carry the authority and power to heal the sick and cast out evil spirits. (Remember that you do not have to petition God for those things; He has already given them to you.)

Of course, our faith is not in following this Five-Step Prayer Model (or any other method); our faith is in God. Nonetheless, this model is a great tool that can help you focus on important principles related to healing and carry them out as you pray for the sick. In Day 4, we will go over the last two steps in this model, which are also important. If you will put this model into practice, I am convinced that you will see an increase in your effectiveness as you minister to the sick.

- Today's Scripture reading: Luke 10:1–24
- Today's reading from *Essential Guide*: pages 228–234

The Berean Approach

1. Why is it a good idea to keep your eyes open most of the time and be watchful when praying for people? What should you ask them to do? (See *Essential Guide* page 229.)

   _____

   _____

   _____

2. What should you do if, after a while, the prayer you are praying is ineffective? (See *Essential Guide* pages 229–230.)

   _____

   _____

   _____

3. I tell the story in today's book pages about the woman who prayed for a blind man for five hours without seeing any results. What basic principle does the story illustrate that is also the bottom line in ministering healing? (See *Essential Guide* pages 230–231.)

   _____

   _____

   _____

4. How long should you continue praying for someone, and why? (See *Essential Guide* page 231.)

   _____

   _____

   _____

5. Why is it good to be transparent about your joy and excitement over what God is doing to heal someone? (It is the reason I express my thanksgiving publicly and loudly enough for the person to hear me; see *Essential Guide* page 231.)

_____

_____

_____

Day 4

IN JESUS' NAME

Randy

Once more Jesus put his hands on the man's eyes. Then his eyes were opened, his sight was restored, and he saw everything clearly.

Mark 8:25

You will not want to skip steps four and five of the Five-Step Prayer Model, *stop and re-interview* and *post-prayer suggestions*. These steps are vital for achieving and maintaining complete healing. In fact, you may need to take step four more than once as you pray for someone. Take it as frequently as necessary to determine what is happening with the person. If the healing is only partial, or if *praying for effect* (step three) is not bringing the desired result, keep stopping to re-interview the person. You may find out something that is pivotal to the healing, or the Holy Spirit may reveal something new that will help direct you to pray more effectively. In today's *Essential Guide* reading I give you several helpful questions you can ask a person in your re-interview. I also discuss how to know when it is time to stop praying, which may or may not coincide with someone's full healing.

After you have worked through steps one through four and your ministry time with a particular person is done, that is the time to take step five and make some *post-prayer suggestions*. Again, I give you several examples in today's reading of appropriate suggestions you can make. The goal is to encourage and exhort the person you were praying for, whatever measure of healing he or she received. It is also a good time to remind the person to thank God for the healing and to go out and tell family and friends about it. Your suggestions are all aimed at helping the person keep his or her healing.

The Five-Step Prayer Model works so well for me! I trust it will work well for you, too, as you become God's co-worker in ministering healing. Remember that this prayer model is not mechanical; it is *relational*. With that in mind, go out and "do the stuff" of living out the Great Commission, doing it all *in Jesus' name*.

- Today's Scripture reading: Matthew 4:23–24; Galatians 6:9–10
- Today's reading from *Essential Guide*: pages 234–240

The Berean Approach

1. What did Jesus do in Mark 8:22–25 when a healing did not happen the first time? What two things does this passage show us? (See *Essential Guide* pages 234–235.)

2. Why is the *stop and re-interview* step so important in the healing process?

3. What does it mean to move more in the spirit of the accuser than in the spirit of the Comforter/Helper? (See *Essential Guide* pages 237–238.) What ways can you think of to avoid doing that?

4. Name some *post-prayer suggestions* you can make in various situations to help people keep their healing. (See *Essential Guide* pages 238–239.)

_____

_____

_____

5. I tell you the story in today's book pages of how God impressed on me the importance of praying *in Jesus' name*. Do you make that a priority when you pray and minister? If you have not done so in the past, how will you incorporate it in the future?

_____

_____

_____

Session 11 Video Guide

1. Randy said about the Five-Step Prayer Model, "It's not about the _____ of it. It's a model that's based on _____."

2. The _____ _____ of this method is, "Do whatever He tells you." . . . _____ is so foundational.

3. Randy said this prayer model "causes us to engage with _____ _____ and to move dependent upon Him and _____ in Him."

4. First Corinthians 3:9 says that we are God's _____. That's what this is about, co-laboring with God, entering into _____ with Him.

5. Randy said when he is praying for someone and God starts to touch one area, "I'm going to _____ the Leader. I'm going to _____ what He's doing, rather than trying to get Him to _____ what I'm saying."

6. The purpose of the _____ is to try to determine the _____ _____ of the illness or the condition.

7. Regarding psychosomatic illness, Randy said, "The fruit of the Spirit can _____ _____ your immune system, but the works of the flesh in Galatians 5 actually _____ and _____ the immune system."

8. Prayers of command are based on _____. They're not _____.

9. You can't cast out a _____, and you can't inner heal an _____ _____, so different ways of praying are important.

10. Pray with your eyes _____ so you can see what the _____ is doing.

11. Praying "in the name of Jesus" is not a talisman, it's not _____, but it is _____ and it is our _____, and so it is important.

12. Randy concluded, "I believe teaching about _____ is our way of saying, 'To win for the Lamb that was slain the _____ of His suffering.'"

OPTIONAL FELLOWSHIP/
WRAP-UP MEETING

I f your *Essential Guide* study group is meeting for this optional Session 12 wrap-up, note that there are no daily readings you need to do or questions you need to answer in preparation for your final session. You should now be finished reading *The Essential Guide* and should have completed this workbook.

You may want to briefly review this study's main points and bring along any final questions you have to that meeting. You also may want to have in mind a healing testimony you can share with your group, or think of some comments about how this study has most helped you understand the healing ministry better. Talk to your group leader(s) for more details about what your final meeting will involve.

VIDEO GUIDE ANSWER KEY

Session 1

1. heal, more, less
2. truth, apply, co-labor
3. knowledge, give
4. Spirit, nervous system
5. big, powerful, heal
6. Experiment, works
7. inbreak, Kingdom
8. power, authority

Session 2

1. effective, resting, flowing
2. worship, exalt, glorify
3. like, worship
4. incorrect, reserved
5. modeling, everyone
6. fire, burning, ignites, people
7. control, shut down
8. change, add
9. impartible, churches
10. cry out, risks
11. contend, pursue
12. lack, excess

Session 3

1. blessing, help
2. difference, doctrines
3. wrote

4. greatness, victory, power
5. meaning, audience
6. medicinal, symbolic, sacramental
7. Scriptures, power
8. salvation, signs, wonders
9. accompany, apostles
10. experience, everybody

Session 4

1. supernatural, 300
2. wind
3. Lord, Savior, healing, miracles
4. born again, supernatural
5. believing believers
6. hear, faith
7. today, today, bedfellows
8. official, wrong, Christ
9. dehumanized
10. blueprint, control, wills
11. victory, 1,000, warfare
12. humble, bridge, wall

Session 5

1. represent, exercise, remove
2. apostolic
3. model, unpacks
4. Kingdom, structure, family
5. relational, dominion, practical
6. here, there

7. redefine, circumstances
8. careless, willed
9. redefine, redefine
10. have, contend, position
11. body, soul, package
12. Righteousness, Peace, Joy

Session 6

1. renewed, encounters, experiences
2. Power, authority
3. catch, wave, power
4. difference, catch, start
5. commission, encounter
6. cracked, leak, filled
7. anointing, gift, grace
8. God, check, wrote
9. Father, connection
10. lead, heart

Session 7

1. confidence, rewarder
2. striving, surrender
3. contrary, superior
4. existence, influence
5. product, Faithful One
6. vital, honest
7. peace, understand
8. quickest, didn't do
9. breakthrough, have, adverse
10. Thanksgiving, underrated
11. small, great

Session 8

1. testimony, prophecy
2. foretells, changes
3. nature, humanity

4. inherit
5. borrow, given
6. do again
7. story, heart
8. qualified, blood
9. testimony, anybody
10. language, unusual circumstances
11. impress, prophesy

Session 9

1. prosperous, lifestyle
2. perfect, heart's, all
3. abundance, life
4. creative influence, solutions
5. Internal, physical
6. teaching, problem, solution
7. finances, relationships, health
8. health
9. Negative thoughts
10. don't, perfect
11. Cry out, serve
12. joy, liberate
13. inheritance, generation

Session 10

1. know, regurgitate, do
2. feel, think, see, read, say
3. recognize, know
4. specific, faith, interpretation
5. numbers, different
6. authentic, sure
7. person, privately
8. strength, ignore
9. ask, risks, victories, mistakes
10. experience, dream

Session 11

1. mechanics, relationship
2. bottom line, Hearing
3. Holy Spirit, trusting
4. co-laborers, partnership
5. follow, bless, bless
6. interview, root cause
7. build up, hinder, compromise
8. authority, presumptive
9. feeling, afflicting spirit
10. open, Father
11. magic, authority, connection
12. healing, rewards

Bill Johnson is a fifth-generation pastor with a rich heritage in the Holy Spirit. Together, Bill and his wife, Beni, serve as the senior pastors of Bethel Church in Redding, California. They also serve a growing number of churches that have partnered for revival. This leadership network has crossed denominational lines, building relationships that enable church leaders to walk successfully in both purity and power.

The present move of God has brought Bill into a deeper understanding of the phrase "on earth as it is in heaven." Jesus lived out this principle by doing only what He saw His Father doing. Heaven was the model for Jesus' life and ministry—and Bill makes it his model as well. Bill demonstrates how recognizing the Holy Spirit's presence and following His lead enables believers to do the works of Christ, destroying the works of the devil.

Bill and his church family regularly see healings in areas ranging from cancer to broken bones to learning disorders to emotional trauma. These works of God are not limited to revival meetings or church services. Bill teaches that believers need to take this anointing into schools, the workplace and their neighborhoods with similar results. We owe the world an encounter with God, he says, and a gospel without power is not the Gospel that Jesus preached. Bill believes that healing and deliverance must become the common expression of this Gospel of power once again.

Bill and Beni have three children and nine wonderful grandchildren. All three of their children are married and involved in full-time ministry with their spouses. To learn more about Bill Johnson, his ministry and his resource materials, visit www.ibethel.org and www.bjm.org.

Dr. Randy Clark, overseer of Global Awakening and the Apostolic Network of Global Awakening (made up of hundreds of churches and hundreds of itinerant ministers), is best known for helping spark the move of God now affectionately labeled "the Toronto Blessing." In the years since, his influence has grown as an international speaker. Noted primarily for revival, healing and impartation, Randy's message is simple: "God wants to use you."

Randy has the unique ability to minister to many denominations and apostolic networks. These have included Roman Catholics, Messianic Jews, Methodists, many Pentecostal and charismatic congregations and the largest Baptist churches in Argentina, Brazil and South Africa. He has also taken several thousand people with him on international ministry teams. His friend and co-author, Bill Johnson, says that the fastest way to increase in the supernatural is to accompany Randy on an international trip. Randy has traveled to fifty countries, and he continues to travel extensively to see that God's mandate on his life is fulfilled.

Randy received his M.Div. from The Southern Baptist Theological Seminary and his D.Min. from United Theological Seminary. He has authored or helped compile over forty books, as well as numerous training manuals and workbooks. In addition, he has published two curriculum sets regarding healing (including this one) and has created master of divinity courses on physical healing at both United Theological Seminary and Regent University Divinity School. He also has developed both the Christian Healing Certification Program and the Christian Prophetic Certification Program online, which have seen over three thousand course enrollments during their first three years.

Randy and his wife, DeAnne, reside in Mechanicsburg, Pennsylvania. They have four adult children, all of whom are married, and five grandchildren. For more information about Randy Clark, his ministry and his resource materials, visit www.globalawakening.com. For information about his online courses, see www.healingcertification.com and www.propheticcertification.com.